In "*What does the Bible say about: Slavery and Freedom?*" Cackie Upchurch provides a helpful guide through this timely topic. Upchurch examines the biblical text in light of today's context, creating a work that is accessible and challenging. For those who wish to move beyond the headlines and to wrestle with issues of inequality, «Slavery and Freedom» provides an excellent biblical foundation on which to begin a conversation.

Laurie Brink, O.P., Ph.D. Professor of New Testament Studies at Catholic Theologica Union

WDBSA Slavery and Freedom should be required reading for everyone running for political office, for every voter, for everyone in ministry leadership, and for all disciples on the faith journey.

More and more today we are realizing that we have a responsibility to know our past, examine the ramifications of our history and strive together on our journey of respecting and celebrating that each human person is made in God's image and likeness. This book is a significant step in understanding our history as God's people. It provides an honest portrayal of the past, explores the use and misuse of Scripture, and examines some of the puzzling passages in Scripture. *WDBSA Slavery and Freedom* challenges us as individuals and communities to stay informed about issues surrounding human dignity; it urges us make sure that the biblical tradition is in dialogue with the real world.

The short discussion questions with each chapter make it ideal for prayerful reflection and conversation by individuals, couples, or small groups on the various forms of slavery around the world, and particularly in the United States.

Janet Schaeffler, O.P.

Drawing not only from the Bible but modern sources such as Martin Luther King and Nelson Mandela, Catherine Upchurch, with clarity and passion, explores the scourge of slavery both in history and in our time. This book is both honest and hopeful. It admits straightforwardly that neither the Hebrew Scriptures nor New Testament condemn slavery. At the same time, it demonstrates that the scriptures include principles that can dismantle slavery in its contemporary manifestations. Those who listen to what Upchurch has presented will find themselves informed and energized to oppose beliefs and practices that continue to diminish human dignity in our world today.

Rev. **George M. Smiga**, St. Mary Seminary and Graduate School of Theology in Wickliffe, Ohio

As we continue to wrestle with the consequences of historic slavery, and the reality of contemporary forms of slavery, this timely book allows us to also wrestle with our Biblical tradition and Biblical approaches to human dignity, slavery, and freedom. And in a time when discussion of these urgent matters is clouded by division, this accessible volume allows communities to reflect together in a way that is both grace-filled and challenging. It will be a valuable resource for adult and campus faith groups, social justice ministries, and individuals seeking renewed energy and transformation.

Justin Huyck, Pastoral Associate and Director Adult Faith Formation, St. Michael the Archangel Parish, Canton, Ohio; and author of *From Home to Home: Finding Meaning in Mobility* and *Baptism: Alive in Christ*

What Does
the Bible
Say About... **?**

Slavery and Freedom

"What Does the Bible Say About...?" Series
Ronald D. Witherup, P.S.S.
Series Editor

What Does
the Bible
Say About... **?**

Slavery and Freedom

Catherine Upchurch

New City Press
Hyde Park, New York

Published by New City Press
202 Comforter Blvd.,
Hyde Park, NY 12538
www.newcitypress.com

© 2021 Catherine Upchurch

Cover design and layout by Miguel Tejerina

Biblical citations are taken from the New Revised Standard Version
© 1989 Division of Christian Education of the National Council of
the Churches of Christ in the United States of America.
Library of Congress Cataloging-in-Publication Data

What does the Bible say about Slavery and Freedom

Library of Congress Control Number: 2021934460

ISBN: 978-1-56548-473-3
ISBN: 978-1-56548-488-7 (e-book)
ISBN: 978-1-56548-697-3 (series ISBN)

Printed in the United States of America

Contents

To those whose quest for
true freedom helps all of us recognize
the image of the divine that we carry.

Series Preface

The Bible remains the world's number one best-seller of all time. Millions of copies in more than two thousand languages and dialects are sold every year, yet how many are opened and read on a regular basis? Despite the impression the Bible's popularity might give, its riches are not easy to mine. Its message is not self-evident and is sometimes hard to relate to our daily lives.

This series addresses the need for a reliable guide to reading the Bible profitably. Each volume is designed to unlock the Bible's mysteries for the interested reader who asks, "What does the Bible say about…?" Each book addresses a timely theme in contemporary culture, based upon questions people are asking today, and explaining how the Bible can speak to these questions as reflected in both Old and New Testaments.

Ideal for individual or group study, each volume consists of short, concise chapters on a biblical theme in non-technical language, and in a style accessible to all. The expert authors have been chosen for their knowledge of the Bible. While taking into account current scholarship, they know how to explain the Bible's teaching in simple language. They are also able to relate the biblical message to the challenges of today's Church and society while avoiding a simplistic use of the biblical text for trying to "prove" a point or defend a position, which is called "prooftexting"—an improper use of the Bible. The focus in these books is on a religious perspective, explaining what the Bible says, or does not say, about each theme. Short discussion questions invite sharing and reflection.

So, take up your Bible with confidence, and with your guide explore "what the Bible says about SLAVERY AND FREEDOM."

Introduction

"Let freedom ring." These three words express a basic human desire, perhaps more aptly, a basic human need. They are words of resolve, determination, and hope. They can be found in country songs and Christian hymns, in civil rights speeches, and in poetry. These words "ring" true because so many in our world know what it is to be trapped in unhealthy and sometimes self-imposed patterns, to be captive to forces beyond one's control, and even to be enslaved physically.

The universal yearning to be free has been behind most political revolutions and movements. Likewise, it is the foundation of almost every treatment plan for those dealing with addictions. And it is certainly a constant theme of the spiritual life as, one by one, sinful impulses and patterns are stripped away and the freedom of God's mercy is embraced.

Freedom, however, requires a consciousness of what binds us, a realization of how we have kept others from experiencing true freedom, and a call for justice for those who are enslaved in systems and policies that fail to honor the dignity of all of creation. In other words, before we can fully enjoy the "freedom of the glory of the children of God" (as St. Paul says in Romans 8:21), we have to identify forms of oppression that enslave so many.

Perhaps most of us have experienced bondage to sin and the accompanying frustration of working to change our behaviors, even as we cling to the mercy of God that cannot be earned. Many of us know firsthand what it feels like to lose control of situations at work or in the civic community, to feel frustrated and trapped in systems that are not life-giving, and do not honor human dignity. Some of us are witnesses to the lack of freedom that comes as a result of little access to education or opportunities. Few of us, however, have experienced actual slavery.

It might be surprising to learn that experts estimate there are between thirty and forty-five million people who are enslaved in the twenty-first century across the globe. The Borgen Project, a global poverty education and advocacy group based in the United States, shares statistics that indicate 78 percent of these are enslaved for labor and 22 percent for sex.[1] We may have believed physical slavery was a distant reality abolished decades and even centuries ago, but the widespread practice of forced labor and human trafficking keeps slavery alive and, sadly, quite well. Yet, the desire and the fight for freedom is also healthy and on the march.

What does the Bible tell us about the experience of slavery? How does the Bible address the issues of injustice that give rise to various forms of slavery? Why is slavery not condemned outright in the Bible? Do justice and human dignity play a role in what the Bible describes as freedom? What other aspects of freedom might we appreciate more deeply in our reading of God's Word?

Religion has been used for centuries to justify attitudes and actions that are sometimes contrary to the very heart of the sacred texts recognized by those same religions. The sacred texts of the Bible have been misused off and on for generations, sometimes to justify the slavery of others and often in attempts to dignify values that are anything but Christian. More often than not, however, the Bible has a way of calling us to a reckoning. It provides an invitation to a truly liberating experience of God, and it shapes our individual and communal conscience, if we let it. Moreover, the Bible provides imagery and language that can help to shape a world that allows true freedom to flourish.

Chapter One

The Bible Tells Me So

Many children would have learned, as I did, the simple song with the familiar refrain, "Yes, Jesus loves me. / Yes, Jesus loves me. / Yes, Jesus loves me. / The Bible tells me so." I grew up feeling confident that what I needed to know for life could be found in the Bible, and that I could trust what I found there. I still know this to be true, but with a deeper appreciation for the kind of truth the Bible imparts.

If we go to the Bible expecting a science lesson, or even a history lesson by twenty-first century standards, we will be disappointed. Ancient peoples did not concern themselves primarily with reporting direct factual data but with uncovering and pondering deeper truths. And so, if we open our Bibles seeking God's truth for our salvation, we will find it. We will be comforted (yes, Jesus does love me, and does love you) and challenged (not by the world's standards, but by God's standards). The Bible can become for us the good news that God is love, and become *in* us the way to life. It matters how we read it, and whether we are open to its deep lessons.

On the topic of slavery and freedom, we come across a bitter irony that cannot and should not be erased. The same Bible that is the source of truth for me, and became the source of hope for Africans enslaved in America, was used by many White slave owners to justify owning slaves.

Numerous writings explore how slavery has been justified by people who profess to be Christian. A few examples will demonstrate some of the arguments:

- The patriarchs and matriarchs of Israel held slaves without the Bible recording a word of disapproval from God. As a specific example, Sarah's slave, Hagar, gave birth to Abraham's first son (Genesis 16).

- The account of the Ten Commandments refer to the treatment of slaves twice (Exodus 20:10, 17) without any condemnation of the practice.

- According to the Gospels, Jesus never addressed the issue of slavery even though it was a widespread institution across the Roman Empire at the time.

- In a letter attributed to Paul, the writer did speak about slavery, but he encouraged slaves to obey their masters, and even gave a spiritual gloss to this command (Ephesians 6:5-9).

Slaveholders and Christianity

Slave owners in seventeenth through nineteenth century America were often seen as upright Christians, shrewd in business, and faithful members of their churches. They either saw no contradiction between their faith and their ownership and treatment of slaves, or they believed they had an inherent right to use forced labor to prosper. Some even believed that their purchase of slaves was part of a larger effort to convert western Africa to Christianity.[2]

Bishop Stephen Elliott, the first and only bishop of the Protestant Episcopal Church in the Confederate States of America, addressed his church convention each year. In his 1861 address, he wrote the following:

> However the world may judge us in connection with our institution of Slavery, we conscientiously believe it to be a great missionary institution—one arranged by God, as he arranges all the moral and religious influences of the world, so that good may be brought out of seeming evil, and a blessing wrung out of every form of the curse. We believe that we are educating those people [African slaves] as they are educated no where [sic] else; that we are elevating them in every generation; that we are working out God's purposes, whose consummation we are quite willing to leave in his hands. . . . We feel sure, that when the whirlwind of passion shall have passed, we shall receive justice at the hands of God's people, being determined, meanwhile, by the grace of God, to defend with the sacrifice of everything, if need be, this sacred charge which has been committed to us. We can not [sic] permit our servants to be cursed with the liberty of licentiousness and infidelity, but we will truly

labor to give them that liberty wherewith Christ has made us all free.[3]

The great irony, of course, is that Bishop Elliott speaks of liberty and freedom for the slaves, but only as far as it goes spiritually.

In recent years we have been made aware that many Catholic religious orders and communities owned slaves in this same period, and that many now respected institutions were built using slave labor. For example, St. Joseph Church in Bardstown, Kentucky, was built in 1819 on the backs of slaves. In the year 2000, that same church was the site of a service of atonement sponsored by three women's religious communities who at one time owned slaves. The Dominicans of St. Catherine, the Sisters of Charity of Nazareth, and the Sisters of Loretto all took part in the service that brought together over four hundred people of all races.[4]

Georgetown University in Washington, D.C., a Jesuit institution, was recently called out for the religious community's ownership of slaves. In an effort to respond to the call for transparency, and to begin to heal the wounds caused by their history, they have launched an effort described on their website as follows:

> Georgetown University is engaged in a long-term and ongoing process to more deeply understand and respond to the University's role in the injustice of slavery and the legacies of enslavement and segregation in our nation.

Through engagement with the members of the Descendant community, collaborative projects and new initiatives, and learning and research, the University pursues a path of memorialization and reconciliation in our present day.[5]

A "long-term and ongoing process" is key to describing efforts required of Christian communities. We have an obligation to dialogue with our past, confront the effects of our history, then and now, and begin to move forward in a way that honors the core of our relationship with God, especially as it is expressed in our relationships with each other.

Is the Bible Clear on Slavery?

We could ease our collective conscience a bit by acknowledging that proponents of institutional slavery misinterpreted the texts. And we would be right on many levels. The Bible has been interpreted or even reshaped to suit our purposes and prop up our opinions on occasion. Its words and stories are quite often taken out of context. To be fair, however, we have to admit that the Bible itself is not always clear on the topic.

On the one hand, Genesis tells us that humans are made in the image and likeness of God. That would imply a certain God-given dignity for all human beings. On the other hand, the stories of Scripture often bypass the likeness of God found in outsiders and enemies of Christians and Jews. For example, Leviticus 25:44-46 indicates that it is perfectly fine to purchase slaves as long as they are not fellow Jews:

> As for the male and female slaves whom you may have, it is from the nations around you that you may acquire male and female slaves. You may also acquire them from among the aliens residing with you, and from their families that are with you, who have been born in your land; and they may be your property. You may keep them as a possession for your children after you, for them to inherit as property. These you may treat as slaves, but as for your fellow Israelites, no one shall rule over the other with harshness.

Does human dignity apply only to God's chosen people? Does it apply only to those who convert and join the believing community? Did slave owners in ancient and in more modern times consider slaves mere property, subhuman, and therefore not endowed with the same dignity?

Likewise, we know from Paul's Letter to Philemon that slavery was an acceptable practice in the early Christian era as well. Although Paul is coaxing Philemon to accept his slave Onesimus as "a beloved brother" (verse 16), Paul falls short of condemning slavery outright.

The commandments found in Exodus 20 and Deuteronomy 5 are a reflection of the covenant relationship that God offers to his people. These laws outline what it means to love God and love neighbor. Jesus himself indicates that the two loves—of God and of neighbor—serve as the center of the law. These loves are the core of what it means to follow him (Matthew 22:34-40).

Somehow, in the course of history, one's "neighbor" came to mean someone who looks and thinks as we do. Even in Jesus' day, this must have been a problem. Jesus' story of the Good Samaritan (Luke 10:29-37) is told to answer the question, "Who is my neighbor?" The neighbor to the traveler who was beaten in the story of Jesus is not a religious leader or a scholar of Israel's law. The true neighbor, in a surprising twist, turns out to be a Samaritan. (We'll hear more about this in chapter three.) It would have been like hearing in the period of United States slavery that a Black slave saved a White child or his mother, or a beaten Black man showed mercy to his owner when trapped in a desperate situation. Jesus' stories, his parables, were often used to shock his listeners into hearing something new. They were, and are, a tool to stir the conscience and upset the status quo.

And yet, the reality is that many church communities simply turned a blind eye and deaf ear to the situation of slaves in the United States. Frederick Douglass, whose life spanned the better part of the nineteenth century, was himself a slave in Maryland. After his escape from slavery he went on to lead abolitionist movements in New York and Massachusetts. He became one of America's most respected voices in the effort to outlaw slavery. His own evaluation of what he saw in White churches led him to write the following:

> Between the Christianity of this land and the Christianity of Christ, I recognize the widest

possible difference—so wide that to receive the one as good, pure, and holy, is of necessity to reject the other as bad, corrupt, and wicked. To be the friend of the one is of necessity to be the enemy of the other. I love the pure, peaceable, and impartial Christianity of Christ; I therefore hate the corrupt, slave-holding, women-whipping, cradle-plundering, partial and hypocritical Christianity of this land. Indeed, I can see no reason but the most deceitful one for calling the religion of this land Christianity.[6]

Douglass's words have a certain bite not just because of his superb language skills. They have teeth because of the clear hypocrisy his words capture, and the raw human experience they lay bare.

Slave owners were also known to use religion as a way to keep their slaves docile and compliant. Slaves were sometimes allowed, sometimes commanded, to attend church services, either from the distance of a balcony or entirely separate, even out in the fields where they were forced to labor. Perhaps the slave owner felt somehow benevolent in this regard. However, we can imagine the effects of a sermon delivered by a White minister on the passage from Ephesians about slaves being obedient to their masters.

Scholars have long been acquainted with a book commonly known as the Slave Bible. In 2017, the only copy of this book in the United States was loaned from Fisk University in Nashville, Tennessee to the newly opened Museum of the Bible in Washington, D.C. In cooperation with a third entity, the National Museum of African American History and Culture, the Slave Bible has reached a growing number of people of all races and religious backgrounds. Its formal title, *Parts of the Holy Bible, selected for the use of the Negro Slaves, in the British West-India Islands*, gives us a clue about its purpose, especially when we recognize that it was edited not by slaves but by slave owners.

The associate curator of Bible and Religion in America for the Museum of the Bible estimates that "about 90 percent of the Old Testament and 50 percent of the New Testament are missing" from the Slave Bible.[7] It was reduced from the Protestant version of almost 1200 chapters to only 232 chapters. What's missing? Any stories or teachings that might have led to revolt among the enslaved. Certainly not every plantation used the Slave Bible, and we are unsure how widely it was distributed. However, the manipulation of the sacred texts of the Old and New Testaments has to be acknowledged and condemned.

Claiming the Bible's Truths

Amazingly, to survive beatings and rapes, to endure daily insults and humiliating treatment, slaves found ways to unearth life in the words of the Bible. The slaves' openness to the sacred writings used, or misused, by Whites to enslave them surely seems strange and paradoxical. But there is much that would give comfort and courage and hope. While most African slaves may have been illiterate, the Bible was always an oral instrument before it became a written one. Slaves, too, learned the stories by listening. Some were already exposed to Christianity by missionaries who had arrived earlier in Africa. Some learned to read and write by using a Bible passed on by a minister meaning to do good or a slave owner imagining it would be beneficial for the slaves to merely have the book in their midst.

Those whose bodies were bought and sold surely held dearly the words that spoke to their own minds and hearts. Perhaps such simple phrases as "The Lord is my shepherd" from Psalm 23 would give comfort. Or a later verse in the same psalm, "Even though I walk through the darkest valley, / I will fear no evil, / for you are with me," could provide courage. The words of Psalm 86:17, "Show me a sign of your favor, / so that those who hate me / may see it and be put to shame," surely crossed the lips of someone oppressed and enslaved.

What is particularly poignant and powerful from this period is the creation of the songs we know as "spirituals." Few, if any, of them credit a specific writer, perhaps because the communities themselves gave rise to these hymns out of their shared experiences. The language and imagery for these songs come directly from the Bible, especially from verses and stories that took on significance for a community bound in slavery and looking for hope. A particular favorite of mine is the hymn, "Wade in the Water":

Wade in the water
Wade in the water children

Wade in the water
God's gonna trouble the water.

Think of the importance of water in the arid Middle East (ancient and contemporary), and the parallel necessity of water in the arid lands of Western Africa, home to so many sold into slavery. There are many associations with water in the Christian tradition, chief among them is baptism. Underlying this sacramental sensibility are the Bible's stories that involve water.

There is the Nile River that provided protection for baby Moses who was hidden there for his survival. It was the Pharaoh's daughter who "troubled the water" and saved the child so that he could grow to manhood (Exodus 2:1-10). Ironically, that same river provided the water necessary for forming clay bricks that became the very heart of Egypt's slave industry.

There is the story of the escape from slavery through the waters of the sea. The same body of water that protected the slaves as they made their way to freedom would crash onto their enemies who pursued them (Exodus 14:10-31). God troubled the water in the cause of freedom.

Past the vastness of the Sinai Desert, the Jordan River served as the portal to the promised land. Before he died, Moses only set eyes on the ribbon of water winding its way through the desert (Deuteronomy 34). It is Joshua who sends the tribes of Israel through the river with the ark of the covenant parting the waters for the people to cross (Joshua 3–4). Centuries later, the Jordan River would become the site of John's baptism of repentance as he prepared the way for Jesus, the Messiah. Even Jesus himself would be baptized in these waters (Mark 1:1-11). And the waters of baptism will forever carry the confidence that God sees his sons and daughters, all of us, as beloved.

God indeed "troubled the waters" in the time of slavery in Egypt, and again in the time of Roman occupation of Israel. God troubled the waters of nations and of souls. Those sold into slavery and held captive to the land and its owners held out hope that God would again trouble the waters.

Centuries later, the songs sung by slaves in America filled the shacks and barns where they lived, and were hummed in the fields and kitchens where they labored. These spirituals gave voice to the conviction of human dignity and the hope for freedom.

For Reflection:

- How has the use of the Bible to justify slavery or other forms of oppression affected your own understanding or acceptance of the Bible? How do you wrestle with contradictions between the truths of the Bible and how they are sometimes used or misused?

- In your experience, how have Christian churches and communities addressed the issue of slavery in our own past? What more could we be doing to acknowledge the past and continue to heal?

Chapter Two

This is Our Story, This is Our Song

There is much that goes into defining the people we become. Some of it is mere accident of birth—being born male or female, living in a temperate or extreme climate, being raised with access to goods and services or not, belonging to a particular race or ethnicity. The list could go on. Sometimes, however, these conditions are reshaped or even shattered by events that also become defining. A child born in poverty may find a teacher who helps to open a new world for her. Travel to other lands might spark scientific interest and discovery and the desire to embrace other cultures. The birth of a child might reorder one's priorities. As individuals, we are in constant interaction with the world around us and given opportunities every day to overcome some new barrier or to be stopped in our tracks.

It is also true that generations and whole peoples are shaped by circumstances and events. My grandparents were part of the generation who knew what it was like to live on rations during the two world wars and a national depression. They had friends who left the safety of home to defend our freedoms on foreign shores, and never returned to their families. Their worldview was shaped by a sense of doing more with less, upholding the freedoms that were hard won, and working hard to make a difference.

Another generation was shaped by different realities— the first human to walk on the moon, the war in Vietnam, the civil rights movement, and the blatant corruption of political leadership revealed during the Nixon era. Thanks to technological advances, all of these events came to us in live reports in our homes. Little boys and girls could dream of becoming astronauts, and of the limitless possibilities that became so obvious in photos sent to us from space. There was hope that a person's skin color would not determine one's value to society or ability to achieve lofty goals. On the flip side, a war that had few filters was also coming into our living rooms replete with body bags and frightened children whose parents were massacred and soldiers who were trying to keep from losing all hope. Daily hearings about political shenanigans that threatened our stability left many people shaking their heads in disbelief.

Our current generation may be shaped by what it means to self-quarantine and shelter in place during a health crisis that spans the globe. Consequently, we may both value the ability to create relationships online and lament the loss of more personal interaction. We may be shaped by the ongoing distress over racial inequality in our country, an issue that some falsely assumed had been resolved but clearly is alive and well in daily interactions and institutionalized policies. And perhaps, concern for the created world that seems to be teetering on the edge of dangerous imbalance will be part of this generation's identity.

Our inner and outer worlds, individually and as a people, are essential components to who we are. They are elements of our identities and signs of how we experience God's interactions with us in the real situations of our lives.

The Exodus Acts as a Focusing Lens

Like most people, our biblical ancestors were molded and shaped by a few key and defining experiences, and their sense of God at work in these events. Paramount among them is the experience of Exodus—slavery and the longing to be free, the great escape, wandering in the Sinai Desert, and entering into a covenant with God who liberated them. Nothing we encounter in the Old Testament was recorded without the events of the Exodus acting as a lens to focus and shape its telling. In fact, a case could be made that the Book of Exodus should appear first in our Bibles since all of Scripture is, in some ways, seen through that lens. God's people repeatedly referenced their combined Egyptian slavery and release as the defining moment of their identity.

For example, the first five books of the Bible are known to Christians as the Pentateuch and to Jews as the Torah. Genesis, Exodus, Leviticus, Numbers, and Deuteronomy each describe in some way the nature of God's relationship with the Hebrews liberated by God from slavery in Egypt in the thirteenth century BC. Although the Book of Genesis stands at the head of the Pentateuch, its position does not mean that it was written first. Rather, Genesis describes first things: God's creation of all that is, the creation of a family (Abraham and Sarah and their descendants) and the creation of a people (the people who will be enslaved, then liberated, and eventually settled in the land of Canaan).

Genesis 1–11 contains what many refer to as the "pre-history" of Israel. This collection of creation stories circulated orally for centuries before being recorded in any written form. All those generations treasured the stories of creation and the fall, of Noah and the great flood, even the tower of Babel. These accounts are evidence that the God who liberated their ancestors in Egypt was the same author of all life and the savior of creation.

The stories of the patriarchs and matriarchs of Israel, filling out chapters 12–50 of Genesis, were recorded in hindsight, centuries after the events described. The writers were people descended from the Hebrew slaves liberated from Egypt. Abraham and Sarah and her maid Hagar, Isaac and Rebekah, Jacob and Leah and Rachel and their maids, all gave birth to generations of people who would one day occupy the land God promised when he called Moses to go to Egypt's Pharaoh and demand that the slaves be set free.

The historical books of the Old Testament often reference the time of slavery and initial freedom as a kind of touchstone as the nation of Israel emerges in the land of Canaan. References abound to the freeing action of God on behalf of those enslaved in Egypt (e.g., Joshua 24:5-13; Judges 2:1; 2 Chronicles 5:10; 7:22). In a particularly strong passage from 1 Samuel 10:17-19, as Israel debates the establishment of a monarchy, God says to the people, "Thus says the Lord, the God of Israel, 'I brought up Israel out of Egypt, and I rescued you from the hand of the Egyptians and from the hand of all the kingdoms that were oppressing you. But today you have rejected your God, who saves you from all your calamities; and you have said, 'No! but set a king over us.'" Every decision seems to be measured against the loyalty Israel owes to the God who saved them from slavery.

The collection of Psalms resounds with the original saving deeds of God in Egypt and in the covenant promises to Moses and the people he led through the desert. At least twenty of the psalms reference or allude to the Exodus, as God's people lift their hearts with the memory of God's active intervention on their behalf. In particular, several of these psalms offer lengthy recollections of the Exodus events, referred to in Psalm 78:4 as "the glorious deeds of the LORD, / and his might, / and the wonders that he has done."

Psalm 105 emphasizes God's fidelity to his promises. By recounting the events of slavery, the sending of Moses to Egypt, the plagues and the slaves' departure from Egypt, the psalmist helps Israel remember that their response was obedience and joy. Psalm 106 uses the story of Exodus to call the people to repentance for their own forgetfulness and disobedience once settled in the promised land. Conversely, Psalm 136 is written as a hymn of thanksgiving for the many ways God acts on behalf of his people, just as he did in Egypt and in the desert wandering.

The use of Exodus themes and language continues into the works of the prophetic writers as they seek to sharpen the conscience of God's people with memories of the covenant God initiated with their ancestors and continues with them (and us). We will explore some of these prophetic passages in future chapters.

The Gospels and other New Testament writings contain Exodus references as well:

- Jesus as the lamb of God, with an understanding that it was lamb's blood on their doorposts that finally freed them from slavery and certain death (John 1:29-36)

- the blood of the lamb or paschal lamb in reference to the death of Jesus (1 Corinthians 5:7; Revelation 5)

- the time of Passover (a remembrance of slavery and liberation) and its association with the time of Jesus' death (Mark 14:12; Luke 22:7)

- comparing the manna in the desert with the bread that is Jesus (John 6)

- the preaching of the apostles recounting God's deeds (e.g., Acts 7:36-41)

- the gift of God's presence in our midst (Hebrews 12).

Indeed, the series of events that we simply refer to as the Exodus is formative for Jews and Christians alike. The experience of slavery in Egypt left an imprint on God's people for generations, as did the freeing action of God through Moses and his brother Aaron and sister Miriam.

Centuries later, the slaves in America (and elsewhere around the globe) would find in the Exodus account echoes of their own experiences.

Slavery and Freedom in the Story of Exodus

The Book of Exodus begins with a conclusion of sorts; it completes the story from Genesis 12–50 of how the Hebrews came to Egypt, and then quickly jumps ahead several generations to their enslavement.

> These are the names of the sons of Israel who came to Egypt with Jacob, each with his household . . . Then Joseph died, and all his brothers, and that whole generation. But the Israelites were fruitful and prolific; they multiplied and grew exceedingly strong, so that the land was filled with them. Now a new king arose over Egypt, who did not know Joseph. He said to his people, "Look, the Israelite people are more numerous and more powerful than we. Come, let us deal shrewdly with them, or they will increase and, in the event of war, join our enemies and fight against us and escape from the land." (Exodus 1:1, 6-10)

The basic story line is familiar to those who read the Bible and those who do not. Cecil B. DeMille's 1956 film, *The Ten Commandments*, drew audiences of all stripes to theaters at the time, and remains a favorite among reruns to this day. The epic retelling of the biblical story focuses on some key elements: the hardships of slavery in ancient Egypt, the return of a favored son, Moses, to do battle with Pharaoh, the one-upmanship between Moses and the Egyptian court magicians, the harrowing escape through dangerous waters, and the meeting of Moses and God on Mount Sinai. But there is much that is missing from the film version—primarily, the invitation to enter into the saga ourselves. We are invited by the sacred words of the Bible to encounter God with Moses and the Hebrew people, and to come away with a deeper sense of who God is and who we are invited to become.

God's people knew the experience of oppression; they felt the jealous anger of a king who felt threatened by their sheer numbers; they cried out to God:

> The Israelites groaned under their slavery, and cried out. Out of the slavery their cry for help rose up to God. God heard their groaning, and God remembered his covenant with Abraham, Isaac, and Jacob. God looked upon the Israelites, and God took notice of them. (Exodus 2:23b-25)

Reading this text in a modern setting, we might be struck wondering why God would need to remember his people. Had God forgotten them, or his promises? However, the verb used here in Hebrew (*zakhar*) is not so much about recollection as it is about relationship. It contains more the sense that God will *act* because of remembrance, because of relationship with his people, the descendants of Abraham whom God promised to make into a great nation (Genesis 12:2-3; 17:3-8). Perhaps by giving voice to their oppression—crying out and groaning—the slaves can allow themselves to expect and accept God's intervention, to trust that God will act.

God is described as remembering, but also as seeing and hearing, taking notice of his people. These same responses are even more vivid in the call of Moses. Having heard his name from the burning bush, having removed his sandals in an awareness of encountering the divine, Moses receives God's message:

> I have observed the misery of my people who are in Egypt; I have heard their cry on account of their taskmasters. Indeed, I know their sufferings, and I have come down to deliver them from the Egyptians, and to bring them up out of that land to a good and broad land, a land flowing with milk and honey, . . . (Exodus 3:7-8)

The God who will fulfill his promises to Abraham's descendants, the God who will liberate them from the oppression of Egyptian slavery *observes* their misery, *hears* their cries, *knows* their sufferings, *comes down* to rescue them, and *brings them up* from despair into a time of hope. This God is actively engaged in the human condition and sets in motion the events that will lead from slavery to freedom.

There are those who would read this story or see it depicted in various art forms and wonder why God would not simply have prevented their oppression, or why God would not have performed an immediate miracle that would sweep them up from Egypt and deliver them to that land of promise. What was the purpose of the plagues? Or the dangerous trek through the waters? Or the harsh conditions of the desert? Or the length of years wandering through a wilderness?

We cannot pretend to know the mind of God, but we can use our imaginations to put ourselves in the situation of those released from slavery and guided to a different land where they could flourish. They had been raised on stories of their ancestors and God's promises to them. The plagues demonstrate to Pharaoh, and even to the Hebrew slaves, that their God is greater than whatever power Pharaoh used to keep them oppressed. Perhaps the long wandering in the desert provides the Hebrews the opportunity to begin shifting from a slave identity to a liberation identity. It takes little to imagine that individual and communal identity would need time to take shape. They had grown used to serving a god (Pharaoh) who either knew nothing of their pain, or knew of it and cruelly exploited them further. It is reasonable to assume that it would take time for the Hebrews to trust that the God revealed to Moses (YHWH, the four letters that represent God's sacred name in Hebrew, not to be pronounced) was different from Pharaoh and the gods of the region, and worthy of their trust.

The story of the Hebrews enslaved in Egypt may seem like ancient history or even folklore but, early on, Jewish ritual life incorporated a way to memorialize the events that created so much of who they came to be (see Exodus

12; 23:15; Leviticus 23:48; Numbers 9:1-5; Deuteronomy 16:1-8). Their experience of slavery was so real, and their experience of God's liberation so tangible, that the yearly Passover meal (or Seder) became a way to relive the events. Participants would embody the experience so fully that each family in every generation who celebrates it has once again entered into its reality. The haggadah is the set of rabbinical instructions for the Seder meal which is a retelling of the historical events that led to freedom. Key from the start is the instruction, "In every generation each individual is bound to regard himself as if he had gone personally forth from Egypt."[8]

The ritual Seder meal is familiar to many people even beyond the perimeters of Judaism. It involves a ceremonial retelling that includes spoken narrative and sung responses, breaking unleavened bread and consuming particular foods that enhance the storyline, raising and consuming glasses of wine, and ritual hand washing. We also enter into these events by reflecting on the realities of oppression in our world, by prayerfully lifting up those people and places where there is a deep need for freedom and self-determination as well as a deep need for God's saving presence. We ponder how our own lifestyles either contribute to captivity in some way or contribute to liberation that honors human dignity.

The story of Exodus is a story of freedom *from* many things, among them freedom from physical bondage, freedom from a society where slaves were not able to worship their God, freedom from fear, and freedom from any self-perceptions of lack of worth. It is also a story of freedom *to* and *for* other things—freedom to shape a new destiny, freedom for worship of the true God, freedom to unite families, freedom for exploring their relationship with God and others.

We know that the time spent in the desert was a time of moving from one way of being to another. It was also a time of rediscovering their God and entering into a relationship that we call covenant. The words of the law that Moses received in his encounter on Mount Sinai (Exodus 20; Mount Horeb in Deuteronomy 5) would govern Israel's relationship with God and with each other. These commands would do so in such a way that God's people could more fully become who they were created to be.

Moving Forward

"Let my people go," the refrain heard so often in gospel spirituals, resonates with every human experience of bondage. It is taken directly from the telling of the Exodus, the words forming a kind of refrain from God that lies at the heart of the story of slavery and freedom, the story that helps to define God's people (see Exodus 5:1; 7:26; 8:16; 9:13; 10:3). And that is a key lesson: those in slavery in Egypt, those at the lowest end of the ladder in terms of status, are God's people. These are the ones with whom God chooses to identify, not just here in the story of Exodus but in the whole of Scripture, and, we believe, in the whole of human history.

Centuries after the events described in Exodus, the Second Vatican Council in the 1960s resurrected several biblical images to describe the church. One such description is the church as "God's People" or the "People of God." The emphasis is clearly on the relationship that God chooses to initiate with us, no matter our status, and the response we can offer as we grow into the image of God in which we are created. The challenge for Israel was fidelity to this call and election, and it is our challenge as well, a reality we will explore in our next chapter.

For Reflection:

- Are there one or two events in your family or parish history that tend to be defining moments? Within these moments could you find the themes of slavery, bondage, or oppression, as well as themes of freedom or liberation?

- Some would say that the Exodus provides a way of understanding or interpreting our spiritual lives through the cycle of slavery or bondage, followed by liberation, followed by a deepening relationship with God (covenant). What other stories from Scripture demonstrate this kind of cycle?

Chapter Three

A Long Way from Home

So much of popular music has been written about the theme of going home: soldiers during wartime yearning for home, college students wanting to return home after their first time away, faraway relatives who wish to be home for the holidays. These types of yearnings are steeped in sentiment, and perhaps a romantic notion about the smells and sounds and even food we associate with being at home.

I discovered when I was a thousand miles from home in college and graduate school that it was not just mom's food or grandma's lemon meringue pie I wanted, or the proximity of my sister and brothers. I wanted my sense of identity to be renewed. I wanted to remember clearly where I had come from and what made me who I was to that point. Being home certainly involves place, but it also involves relationships and the values shaped by those relationships. For that reason, we can be at home in any number of places, and we might feel exiled just as easily.

Covenant Relationship Creates Home

The Hebrew people were not at home in Egypt, at least not in a way that provided the security we usually associate with home. Moses led them out from a place of shared experience but not a deeply shared identity; Egypt was not home. Home for them would always be in the heart of the relationship God formed with them in the desert, carved out in a special way in the promised land.

God's people survived the wilderness of Sinai for forty years (Joshua 5:6), which is a wonderful way of indicating they survived as a wandering people a long time, more than a generation. Along the way, they encountered hardships and they too fell back into the somewhat romantic notion that they wanted to return to the security they knew in Egypt. At least there they had food (Exodus 16:1-3). In those years, God not only provided manna and quail; God also provided the opportunity to move spiritually and mentally from slavery to freedom. They moved from adhering to the commands of the Pharaoh who did not know them in any meaningful way, to responding to the God who created them and loved them. In those years they learned to be at home in covenant with the God who liberated them.

One way to understand that covenant relationship is to begin with a look at the ten commands that were revealed to Moses in his encounter with God in the Sinai (Exodus 20:2-6; Deuteronomy 5:6-11). These commands are intended to be life-giving and community-forming. They set the divine standard for life within the community of God's people and beyond that community as well.

In both biblical accounts, the commandments were preceded by this reminder: "I am the LORD your God, who brought you out of the land of Egypt, out of the house of slavery" (Exodus 20:2; Deuteronomy 5:6). The context for Israel's obedience to God was the experience of liberation. That foundational experience is not confined to that original generation but to all who would follow.

The first three commands spell out what it means to love God—to love only God and no others, to protect the name of God by never taking it in vain, and to set aside the Sabbath to honor God. The reason for the Sabbath rest referred to in the third of these commands is twofold: to imitate God resting on the seventh day of creation (Exodus 20:11), and to remind themselves that they were once slaves in need of liberation (Deuteronomy 5:15). Their identity would always be flavored by the experience of slavery, not so much as a burden or an open wound but as a reality that bound them to one another and to the God who freed them.

The final seven commands revealed to Moses deal with love of neighbor—honoring father and mother, protecting the sanctity of life, refusing to misuse others sexually, recognizing the right of others to their property, being honest in relationships, safeguarding marriage relationships, and being grateful for one's own possessions and not covetous of others' possessions. These seven commands are a way of embracing God's qualities in daily living.

Centuries later Jesus would be asked by the Pharisees, in an attempt to trip him up, to identify which commandment in the law is the greatest (Matthew 22:35-40; Mark 12:28-31; see also Luke 10:27a). His response is direct: "'You shall love the Lord your God with all your heart, and with all your soul, and with all your mind.' This is the greatest and first commandment. And a second is like it: 'You shall love your neighbor as yourself'" (Matthew 22:37-39).

Taken as a whole, all ten commands provide the framework for what it means to live as a free people. While originally revealed to the Hebrews as they journeyed toward a land they could call home, they provide the underpinnings of what it means to be at home for any of us. The summary provided by Jesus helps us to focus on the overall and deep intent of the ten commands. When we focus on each of them individually, like a litmus test, it can give way to legalism rather than embracing the law of love.

In the Jewish tradition, the ideal of loving God and neighbor is expressed in laws, especially the Ten Commandments. Additionally, there are many developments of these laws found throughout the Pentateuch (the Torah, or first five books of our Bible), especially in the books of Leviticus and Deuteronomy. There is legislation governing all aspects of raising cattle, planting and harvesting crops, every detail of religious ritual and appropriate offerings, and all kinds of provisions for household relationships. After perusing these books today, we might argue that as the Hebrews settled in the land of God's promise, they "over-legislated" their people or that they robbed the law of its spirit. However, their intention was to have the original divine commands permeate every aspect of the precious gift of life and freedom they had been given, the free gift of being at home with God.

What a surprise, then, to find that God's people themselves kept slaves. And, apparently, they saw little conflict between this practice and the command to live in a covenant of love with God and neighbor.

Slavery Persists

The initial fervor of commitment that greeted Moses and his pronouncement of God's covenant did not last long. "Everything the LORD has spoken, we will do" (Exodus 19:8) must have begun to feel restrictive. It required so much trust. It surely would have put the Hebrews at odds with the cultures and political realities of their neighbors as they settled in the land of Canaan.

When the freed slaves finally crossed the Jordan River at the border of Egypt, there were, of course, already people living in the land of Canaan. While Israel's dealings with these native peoples may have been typical of the time, it did not embody fully the characteristics of the commandments. Some may point to a passage such as Deuteronomy 7:1-2 as proof that God did not intend for the Hebrews to treat outsiders with respect. There it states that God allows the defeat of the land's occupants, and specifies, "Make no covenant with them and show them no mercy." The Hebrews who entered Canaan understood the land to be theirs by God's design and intervention; it was the land God promised to them. There would come a time, however, when Israel would see its covenant with God in a broader way, including a responsibility to be a "light for the nations" (Isaiah 49:6; 56:6-8; see also Isaiah 55:5; Zechariah 8:20-23).

Slavery among God's own people was not uncommon, another instance that with the benefit of hindsight contradicts the spirit of the commandments. Exodus 21:1-6, a passage immediately following the giving of the law, assumes the Hebrews would purchase slaves from among the poorer families of their own ranks. In that instance, a male slave was to be set free after six years, and he was allowed to take his wife with him if he and she were married prior to being purchased. However, if a man married while a slave, his wife and children remained the property of the slave owner. The man could leave in his seventh year or, if he chose to stay with his family who remain the master's property, his ear was pierced with an awl in the sight of God, and he and his family were to remain slaves forever. One wonders what part of this constitutes loving God and neighbor.

It gets more complicated and compromising if the slave was a daughter who was sold into slavery by her father. She did not have the same rights as males sold into slavery (Exodus 21:7-11), and of course this difference between the treatment of females and males was not unique to the institution of slavery. Young female slaves were often taken as wives, perhaps made part of a harem for the master. If he grew tired of her ("if she does not please her master") she could be sold to another, but not to foreigners. Sometimes young women who were sold into slavery were designated as wives for the master's son. The only way a slave wife was allowed to leave in this arrangement was if the son took another wife and then withheld food, clothing, or conjugal rights from the slave who was his wife.

Deuteronomy 15:12-18 acknowledges that a Hebrew person may sell himself into slavery, presumably to settle a debt or provide for daily needs. After six years the slave was to be freed but would not leave empty-handed. "Provide liberally out of your flock, your threshing floor, and your wine press, thus giving to him some of the bounty with which the LORD your God has blessed you" (Deuteronomy 15:14). Leviticus 25:35-55 outlines several scenarios where one's relatives may sell themselves because of poverty. In such cases, the masters were to treat their kin differently than the slaves they purchased from other nations who lived in their midst. Relatives who were purchased were entitled to borrow money from their master without interest, purchase food at fair prices, and be released in the jubilee (or seventh) year.

In both Deuteronomy and Leviticus, the overriding reason for freeing slaves, or treating indentured relatives differently from foreign slaves, was their own ancestral experience of being freed themselves: "Remember that you were a slave in the land of Egypt, and the LORD your God redeemed you" (Deuteronomy 15:15a; see also Leviticus 25:38, 42, 55).

Perhaps it is time to revisit that notion of home. A slave in ancient Israel, even a member of one's tribe or family, may have had housing for a time but had no real home outside of God's covenant care. A slave or indentured relative could only hope for a master who might adhere to the laws that allowed freedom after six years of labor. Perhaps a slave might also hope for a master with a long memory of God's care, and whose heart would continue to be transformed by the overriding principle of loving God and neighbor.

These scenarios call to mind the story that in the Gospel of Luke comes right after Jesus identifies loving God and loving neighbor as the greatest commandment. A scholar of the law asks Jesus to identify the "neighbor" who is to be loved (Luke 10:20-37). Jesus answers with the now familiar, but at the time shocking, story of the Good Samaritan. A traveler is robbed, beaten, and left for dead lying in a ditch along a well-traveled road. Both a priest and a Levite pass by without coming to his assistance; in fact, they cross to the other side of the road. It is a Samaritan, a man whose very nationality put him at odds with Israel, who reaches out to help. And this Samaritan goes so far as to care for the injured man overnight and then pay the innkeeper to continue his care. Jesus says the "neighbor" was "the one who treated him with mercy." The neighbor is not only the one who is most like us. The neighbor is the one who shows mercy, the one who, regardless of status or language or skin color, embodies the merciful love of God.

And lest we feel a bit smug imagining the failures and shortcomings of our Jewish ancestors, consider that slavery persisted into the New Testament era. Letters attributed to Paul often include sets of instructions about community life in the early Christian communities. Slavery continued to be an acceptable practice. In Colossians 3:22, and Ephesians

6:5, we read "Slaves, obey your earthly masters in everything, not only while being watched and in order to please
them, but wholeheartedly, fearing the Lord." And while
Ephesians adds a verse advising masters to stop threatening
their slaves, there is certainly no condemnation.

Culturally acceptable practices such as settling debts
through indentured servitude, or selling daughters to create
alliances or accumulate wealth, were just that—culturally
acceptable. And in many parts of the world today, these
practices and others still persist as forms of slavery. As an
example, a woman in her early twenties left her home in
a small town in Uzbekistan in hopes of finding work in
a larger city. Without much education or experience she
was unable to find work until offered a job waitressing in
yet another city. As it turns out, she was shipped out to
Dubai along with several other young women and sold into
sex trafficking. For eighteen long months she was expected
to earn top dollar for her "owners," until she finally asked
a police officer to arrest her. Shame followed her back to
her home country and it was years before she felt at home
enough to trust those who helped to turn her life around.[9]
Whether such practices go unchallenged might well
depend on whether we see the difference between living by
the covenant and living by culturally acceptable standards.

Forgetting One's History

Another slice of ancient history will illustrate just how far Israel had wandered from home, either forgetting or not fully understanding the covenant. Israel's twelve tribes were united under a monarchy that lasted about a century, comprising the reigns of Kings Saul, David, and Solomon. While David is often depicted as the ideal king, Solomon was the one responsible for the largest expansion of territory, regional power, and construction, including the Temple in Jerusalem (see 1 Kings 4–11). One scriptural tradition attributes Solomon's undoing to the influence of his foreign wives and their gods. In his later years he built shrines to their gods and engaged in offering sacrifice at those places: "So Solomon did what was evil in the sight of the LORD, and did not completely follow the LORD, as his father David had done" (1 Kings 11:6). Solomon broke the covenant promise to love God.

Solomon also broke the promise to love neighbor. After Solomon's death, Jeroboam (a former aide to Solomon) challenged Solomon's son Rehoboam to "lighten the harsh servitude and the heavy yoke" Solomon had placed on his people (1 Kings 12:1-4). When Rehoboam's demands were not met, a united Israel was no more. Two kingdoms emerge, Israel to the north and Judah to the south. So how did Solomon violate the dignity of his own people? To prosper his plans for grandeur, Solomon had imposed heavy taxes on Israel's citizens (1 Kings 4:7-19) and employed forced labor for his building projects (1 Kings 5:27-32).

Surely we cannot miss the irony: the very people whose slavery almost destroyed them centuries earlier were enslaved once again, not by a foreign leader but by their own king. The very leaders whose role was to communicate God's continuing presence with Israel imitated foreign leaders when they enslaved their own people.

The Oppressed as Oppressors

It seems that the moral lesson is true: without true transformation of the experience, the oppressed are sometimes likely to become oppressors. We see this dynamic throughout history when old grievances from periods of war are settled with cruelty as history moves forward. We know of abusers having been abused themselves at a young age. And while this principle may apply to individuals, it is also true for communities.

Slavery and its ancestor, racism, are forms of oppression that survive only in a community that tolerates them. While individuals are in need of transformation, so are communities that foster hate, tolerate oppression, turn a blind eye, or refuse to recognize the disease that exists there.

So often our idea of human rights is shaped around the individual and his or her freedoms. This is perhaps a good beginning. The Bible certainly upholds the dignity of the human person. We are nourished with a sense of our own value in the eyes of God—from the astounding truth that humans are made in the image and likeness of

God (Genesis 1:27) to the teaching of Jesus that we are worth more than a flock of sparrows, and every hair on our heads is counted (Matthew 10:29-31). This personal sense of worth is essential to our relationship with God and to our working and being in the world. But the Bible invites us to move forward with that sense of personal worth into an appreciation of and commitment to the common good.

Frequently, individual freedoms and the common good are depicted as being pitted against one another in some kind of fight to the death. However, if we see the larger community as a people imbued with dignity, then our personal freedoms are often *not* at odds with the common good. Matthew Briand, SJ, wrote about the dynamic between the two interests during the time of pandemic in 2020. His insight applies in this discussion as well. Briand states, "The conflict between these different notions, I would argue, arises from thinking of freedom solely as a political right. But if we understand our freedom primarily as a gift from God, then the opposing sides in this conflict are not inherently opposed, but can be recognized as different expressions of a shared desire, namely to love."[10] The common ground is love, which is God's gift, and the birthplace and protector of human dignity and freedom.

While the pages of our Bibles are filled with stories of human failure to embrace the law of love, there are also pages filled with the call to return to the covenant relationship with God and others. We can find in the Scriptures the courage to reform, the grace to repent, and the resolve to act justly.

For Reflection:

- Why is it important for us as Jews and Christians to know our ancestral stories and acknowledge the sin we find there? What difference does it make in our own discussions about our faith and our practices?

- What habits do you practice that keep the law of loving God and loving neighbor ever before you? In what practical ways are these two aspects of love front and center in your family? In your church community?

Chapter Four

Created in God's Image

Have you noticed that it is often only with time, lived experience, and deeper reflection that we come to appreciate lessons that were right there in front of us all along? Or that what we learned as children, appropriate as it was for our young ages, tends to expand and deepen with the benefit of maturity? We revisit early lessons and see them with a wider lens. Part of this is because of the realities of human development. What we can comprehend and digest as children is somewhat limited by the restricted breadth of our experiences. As we mature, our brains develop, our experiences broaden, and our ability to think critically improves.

It occurs to me that a similar expanded learning happens in other settings, such as what we learn about ourselves spiritually throughout our lifetimes, and what we learn about what God has revealed. Thankfully, the lessons of faith we learn as children ground us, but do not leave us at that level of maturity. As we develop and mature, so our faith must do the same, individually and as a community.

God's people received instruction in the form of the Ten Commandments, for example, and agreed heartily to obey them. But it took generations for the community of faith (whether Jewish or Christian) to mature enough to deal with the more challenging aspects of obedience to God. Is loving neighbor restricted simply to the neighbor who looks like us? Speaks like us? Believes like us? Is the dignity of the human person reserved only for people who share our religious convictions? Or skin color? Or ethnicity?

Just as the individual believer must reexamine and recommit to her or his beliefs over time, the community of faith must do the same. It is that "reexamining" part of the process where the work of maturing as a community of faith happens. As we examine and reexamine what the Bible does and does not say about slavery, hopefully we can acknowledge an evolution of understanding of what God reveals in Scripture. Israel's prophets served in such a capacity for their ancient communities. They revisited the covenant commands and challenged the community and its political and religious leaders to grow in understanding of the implications of God's law. Their words are part of the continued revelation of God. Jesus, too, revisited the cornerstone of his tradition (loving God and neighbor), and his teachings also served to stretch his curious listeners and his ardent followers.

But let us be clear. Do the prophets directly condemn the common practice of slavery? No. Can we find words of Jesus that directly condemn slavery? No. Does that mean the case is closed? No. In a broader and deeper way, the Bible condemns the attitudes and behaviors that lead to slavery. The Bible speaks with divine authority about human dignity, which is essential to freedom. Yet, it has taken a very long time for the prophetic words of the Old

Testament and of Jesus to truly challenge the accepted cultural practices surrounding slavery.

The Prophetic Tradition:
Reexamining What We Thought We Knew

In some circles today, the ancient words of the biblical prophets are read as simple predictions of the future. Whether intended or not, this way of reading the prophets reduces the power of their critique of society. And it ignores the prophets' role in calling their own religious communities to live up to the demands and freedoms of the covenant.

How about an example? The book of the prophet Amos opens with a series of speeches condemning the practices of the nations surrounding Judah and Israel. We can almost imagine the religious people of Judah and Israel smugly rejoicing that the prophet is giving their neighbors their comeuppance. But Amos then turns to a critique of Judah, "because they have rejected the law of the LORD, / and have not kept his statutes" (Amos 2:4). Next in line is Israel, "because they sell the righteous for silver, / and the needy for a pair of sandals— / they who trample the head of the poor into the dust of the earth, / and push the afflicted out of the way" (Amos 2:6-7). This is a pretty harsh assessment that clearly tells us the prophets had more on their minds and hearts than predicting a distant future.

Biblical prophets often spoke in first person voice such as "I say to you . . ." Their words, however, are the words of God through them. Their words are intended to tear down in society what is counter to God's covenant so that the covenant can be freed of preconceptions. That covenant of loving God and loving neighbor is the measuring rod applied to religion, politics, family life, and personal interactions. However, the prophet, in God's name, does not just tear down and leave the community without hope. There is room for repentance. There is room for renewal. There is room for restoration.

The prophet, in the words of Old Testament scholar Walter Brueggemann, both criticizes and energizes.[11] This work is done in the context of political and military expansion by the larger powers of Assyria, Babylon, Persia, and then Rome. In the history of Israel, the prophets were most active after the united monarchy, under Kings Saul, David, and Solomon, began to crumble. This was a time when small nation-states of the region struggled to maintain their identity as well as their borders. It was during these centuries of changing political fortunes that God called the prophets to speak to his people, to remind Israel and Judah who they were and whom they worshiped.

Living out the covenant never happens in a vacuum. These were centuries filled with political upheaval, military battles, and strained loyalties. Within Judah and Israel there is evidence of great disparity between the haves and the have-nots, growing distrust of the monarchy that appeared to have abused its power, and little respect for justice in daily dealings with one another. If that sounds familiar, it should. We may notice the same characteristics

in our modern world. That's why, even though the prophets' words are centuries old, they are relevant in every age.

What do the prophets have to say that is relevant to
dismantling the practice of slavery, be it in the form of
human trafficking, racism, indentured servitude, or dehumanizing addictions? How does their critique tear down
the foundations of injustice, and how does their vision help
direct God's people toward a more just and loving society,
a society awash in true freedom?

Human Dignity is the Essential Truth

There are many factors that allow slavery to be acceptable
and even to flourish:

- justifying the use of free labor to build a flourishing
  economy (for some but not for all)

- believing that the destitute are better off in slavery
  than simply starving

- asserting that because slavery has existed for centuries
  it cannot be undone.

At the basis of it all is denying the dignity of the human
person if that person is different from us, different in skin
color, ethnic background, gender, belief systems, economic
status, and so forth. The minute we focus on those around
us as "other" than us, we can easily slip into debasing the
"other." As an example in our own day and time, major

sporting events serve to feed our interest in competition and pride, but at the same time they are often the very venues where sex trafficking, hidden for many years, is most prevalent. Additionally, to construct the venues for these events, many unscrupulous employers exploit the needy in the interest of supplying cheap labor. Enticed by ingenuous offers, foreign workers are often promised high pay only to arrive and find low pay, poor housing, and little possibility of earning enough money to return home.

Let's return to the brief passage from Amos 2:6-7 where the prophet condemns the sins of Israel: selling the righteous for silver and the needy for a pair of sandals, trampling the head of the poor into the dust, and pushing the afflicted out of the way. Amos is describing a way of life that had become commonplace in his time, a way of life where the haves were able to ignore the humanity of those who could not fend for themselves. The desires of one group (for wealth and comfort) had become more important than the needs of another group.

A little later, in Amos 8:6, the prophet repeats the charge, and adds to his condemnation that Israel's wealthy are even "selling the sweepings of the wheat." In the ancient world when all crops were harvested by hand, the first pass through the fields at harvest time could not possibly remove every shred of the crop. Likewise, some of what was harvested inevitably ended up on the ground to be swept up later. Israel observed the practice of gleaning, that is, allowing the poor to gather what they could after the initial harvest. In fact, it is part of Mosaic law:

When you reap your harvest in your field and forget a sheaf in the field, you shall not go back to get it; it shall be left for the alien, the orphan, and the widow, so that the LORD your God may bless you in all your undertakings. When you beat your olive trees, do not strip what is left; it shall be for the alien, the orphan, and the widow. When you gather the grapes of your vineyard, do not glean what is left; it shall be for the alien, the orphan, and the widow. (Deuteronomy 24:19-21; see also Leviticus 19:9-10; 23:22.)

When Amos, speaking for God, condemns Israel's landowners for selling even the sweepings of the wheat, he is calling out their violation of the law. He is also, more importantly, underlining that the poor and the wealthy alike share a common humanity, even when the poor are foreigners and not part of the covenant community by birth or by choice. Access to food crops is essential to human survival as well as human dignity.

The prophet Isaiah laments how justice has been perverted and human dignity ignored when he says:

Ah, you who make iniquitous decrees,
who write oppressive statutes,
to turn aside the needy from justice
and to rob the poor of my people of their right,

that widows may be your spoil,
and that you may make the orphans your prey!
(Isaiah 10:1-2)

Slavery cannot stand without devaluing human persons. Human trafficking, whether it be children or poor workers desperate for money, survives when human dignity is ignored. So, the very foundation of dismantling slavery is accepting and honoring the truth of human dignity.

The prophets were steeped in the ancient sacred stories of their tradition. They would have been well aware of the truths laid out in what is now the first book of the Bible. In the first account of creation, after fashioning places and creatures to fill those places, God creates the human person. The writer of Genesis states in simple words this profound and foundational truth: "So God created humankind in his image, / in the image of God he created them; / male and female he created them" (Genesis 1:27).

The belief that the human person carries within himself or herself the very image of God is the basis of all of our interactions. Simply put, we believe that where the human person is, God is. Others have an encounter with our God when they have an encounter with us. Treating others with violence, ignoring their basic rights, and demeaning their very existence reveals something about the idea of God we carry within us. Surely in such encounters with others, we reveal that our idea of God is much too small, even perverted.

Recall that in many ways, as we already said, the experience of slavery in America included exposure to carefully selected passages of Scripture that tended to uphold the slave owner's rights and viewpoints. It is little wonder that slaves who were force-fed a diet of a warped kind of Christianity were hesitant to embrace the idea of God revealed by their slave owners. Occasionally a preacher would leave behind a Bible, not so much for the slaves to read as to remind them of their masters. Little did many slave owners know that the Bible became the book of choice for learning to read, even after long hot days and nights working fields and cooking over hot stoves. Once exposed to the breadth of Scripture, slaves were more inclined to embrace the God who they discovered freed the Hebrews from slavery in Egypt, the God who spoke through the prophets to condemn hypocrisy and neglect of the poor. They found support for their own worth and dignity within the words of Scripture even if their owners did not.

How we treat others flows from recognizing our own dignity and that of others. It is also a reflection of how we treat God, since we carry within us God's image. Israel's prophets highlight this dimension of being made in God's image every time they remind God's people to care for the poor, the widow, the orphan, and the stranger. These are not acts of benevolent pity for others who are somehow "less than" themselves. These are acts that reveal God's priorities, what the church has come to call God's preferential option for the poor. The phrase "preferential option for the poor" was first used in a 1968 letter from Father Pedro Arrupe, the superior general of the Jesuits.[12] It has become common in Catholic social teaching to use the phrase when describing the overwhelming body of Scripture and church teaching that demands attention and care for those at the margins of society. But this is not simply a matter of the "haves" caring for the "have-nots." There is a mutuality that is essential.

Consider the scene on the road to Damascus described in the Acts of the Apostles. Armed with the intent of doing harm to Jesus' followers, Saul (later known as Paul) discovers how connected our treatment of others is to our treatment of God. Thrown to the ground by a flash of light, he encounters the risen Lord who says to him, "Saul, Saul, why do you persecute me?" [Saul] asked, "Who are you, Lord?" The reply came, "I am Jesus, whom you are persecuting" (Acts 9:4-5). What some refer to as Saul's moment of conversion, or his new calling, changed the way he saw Jesus. He came to understand in a profound way that Jesus was the Messiah, the anointed of God. Saul's conversion did not stop there; it also changed the way he saw Jesus' followers, and the way he saw himself.

That's the thing about coming to an awareness that changes our world—it transforms all aspects of our world, including ourselves, if we allow it. The slave owner *and* the slave are made in God's image. Believing in the dignity of the human person is good news for both the slave and the owner, because it has the power to liberate the oppressed and the oppressor. It has the power to remind each that they are first and foremost human beings, not owners and property.

In more recent times, the story of South Africa's Nelson Mandela could serve as a lesson for us. Racial segregation had been practiced in the country since the early part of the twentieth century, with the minority White population in control of government and land, and the general population, largely Black, banned from participation in the system of rule. This practice, known as apartheid, was codified in 1948 and officially sanctioned political, legal, educational, and economic discrimination against non-Whites. One of the leaders of the movement against apartheid was Nelson Mandela who was arrested several times and spent a total of twenty-seven years in prison, eighteen of those years in hard labor on desolate Robben Island. Finally released in 1990 as apartheid was ending, Mandela had every reason to harbor resentment and hatred but instead demonstrated a depth of forgiveness and sense of his own dignity. Mandela wrote:

> Even in the grimmest times in prison, when my comrades and I were pushed to our limits, I would see a glimmer of humanity in one of the guards, perhaps just for a second, but it was enough to reassure me and keep me going. Man's goodness is a flame that can be hidden but never extinguished.

> It was during those long and lonely years that my hunger for the freedom of my own people became a hunger for the freedom of all people, white and black. I knew as well as I knew anything that the oppressor must be liberated just as surely as the oppressed. A man who takes away another man's freedom is a prisoner of hatred, he is locked behind the bars of prejudice and narrow-mindedness. I am not truly free if I am taking away someone else's freedom, just as surely

as I am not free when my freedom is taken from me. The oppressed and the oppressor alike are robbed of their humanity.[13]

Jesus demonstrates the value of the human person very well in so many encounters described in the Gospels. He frees the adulterous woman from her own self-defeating behavior, and at the same time teaches her accusers that all people are in need of God's mercy (John 8:2-11). The stoning becomes an opportunity for both the woman and her accusers to discover their dignity. When Jesus encounters Zacchaeus in Jericho (Luke 19:1-10), he focuses not on the tax collector's reputation of underhandedness but gives him the dignity of looking him in the eye and inviting himself to dinner. In the process, Jesus is offering the crowds the opportunity to put aside their prejudice and discover their worth as well.

The poignant story of the man who asks Jesus what he must do to inherit eternal life (Mark 10:17-22) also demonstrates the dignity of the human person. The man tells Jesus that he keeps all of the commandments but knows there is more. Jesus tells him to sell what he has, give to the poor, and then come and follow him. We tend to focus on the fact that the man goes away sad. But the jewel is perhaps right in the middle, just after he has told Jesus he is obedient to the law. The Scripture text says, "Jesus, looking at him, *loved him* and said [to him] . . ." (italics added). That love that Jesus has for the man honors his dignity and encourages him to take the next step. Mind you, we are not privy to what the rich man may have done eventually.

In case we simply want the affirmation that human beings are precious to God, we can hear Jesus say to those who will listen that the very hairs on their head are counted, and their worth surpasses a flock of sparrows (Matthew 10:30). What human being can resist the love God expresses in his faithfulness and his care? Surely slaves of previous centuries and slaves in our world today need to be reminded that they are precious to God, that what happens to them matters to God. As hard as that can be to believe when in the midst of dehumanizing oppression, it is a truth we acclaim. It is a truth that the oppressed and the oppressor need to hear as part of the continued work of conversion.

For Reflection:

- In recent years, more attention is given to the realities of injustice that are systemic, that is, injustice that is ingrained in the fabric of our society's institutions. What issues of injustice have captured your attention as being part of how things work in our culture? How are these injustices being addressed in the public square? In your experience of church?

- If we are called to uphold human dignity in situations of oppression, how does that look? What does human dignity offer the oppressed? And what does it require of the oppressor?

Chapter Five

Do Unto Others

Americans must acknowledge that slavery is a disgraceful chapter in our nation's history. Coming to a critical mass in the nineteenth century, the issue sparked a civil war. Its causes and effects still linger in the air as we determine how to preserve this tragic chapter without nostalgically glorifying it on the one hand, or ignoring it on the other. Even as many White Christians at the time of the war used their religion to justify slavery, there were others who were raising serious questions. The voices of two sisters will serve as an example.

Prophetic Voices from the Pews

Angelina Grimké, whose life spanned three quarters of the nineteenth century, was a southern-born Quaker. She and her sister, Sarah, were both actively engaged in the abolitionist movement in the United States. They drew upon the tenets of their faith to condemn the practice of slavery and to dismantle its support among other Christians. Both women printed pamphlets that became widely circulated in the late 1830s.

For her part, Angelina addressed her words to southern women who were slave owners or the wives of slave owners. She acknowledged that Christ did not condemn slavery in direct language, but pointed out that owning and mistreating slaves blatantly ignored the golden rule laid out by Christ in the Gospels. In Matthew 7:12, it is stated in this way: "In everything do to others as you would have them do to you." In order to ignore this teaching, owners had to consider slaves as possessions rather than human beings who bear the image of God.

Grimké's words were meant to stir the conscience of her female audience, and to prod them to think and pray. She wanted to help them see how they devalued the human person by being party to slavery in their homes and in the fields of their husbands. She wrote:

> Let every slaveholder apply these queries to his own heart: Am I willing to be a slave—Am I willing to see my husband the slave of another—Am I willing to see my mother a slave, or my father, my white sister, or my white brother?[14]

Surely Grimké's questions would have hit home with many women if they allowed themselves to ponder a legitimate answer. However, if her audience objected with the common argument that their White families were not suited to slavery as were those born into slavery, Grimké insisted:

> It has been justly remarked that 'God never made a slave,' he made man upright; his back was not

made to carry burdens as the slave of another, nor his neck to wear a yoke, and the man must be crushed within him, before his back can be fitted to the burden of perpetual slavery.[15]

"The man must be crushed within him." Angelina Grimké lays bare the truth that human beings brought to this country from parts of Africa were not only forced to provide labor but were robbed of their very humanity. This is true also of those brought here as indentured servants from parts of Europe, promised a new lease on life only to be bound to a landowner with almost impossible requirements to buy their freedom.

If challenging the women whose plantations flourished on the backs of slaves was not enough, imagine the sting of a lay woman challenging clergy to examine themselves and their leadership. Angelina's sister, Sarah, printed and circulated a pamphlet admonishing southern clergy who defended slavery in the name of God. In *An Epistle to the Clergy of the Southern States*, she writes powerfully of how easily the clergy have reduced slaves to things, and in the process are not serving God but the prince of darkness:

In the image of God created he man. Here is marked a distinction which can never be effaced between a man and *a thing*, and we are fighting against God's unchangeable decree by depriving this irrational and immortal being of those inalienable rights which have been conferred upon him. He was created a little lower than the angels, crowned with glory and honor . . . but slavery has seized with an iron grasp this God-like being, and torn the crown from his head. Slavery has disrobed him of royalty, put on him the collar and the chain, and trampled the image of God in the dust.[16]

These two women continue the biblical prophetic tradition. They speak from the heart of the covenant God has made with the human race, a covenant of loving God and neighbor. They speak from the conviction that every person is made in the image of God, without regard for color or nationality or economic status. They speak with courage in the face of enormous opposition to their teaching. Not only do the Grimké sisters challenge a foundational structure for slavery (viewing slaves as possessions and not as humans), in the tradition of the prophets they also offer hope through repentance. Sarah Moore Grimké writes:

How long the space now granted for repentance may continue, is among the secret things which belong to God, and my soul ardently desires that all those who are enlisted in the ranks of abolition may regard every day as possibly the last, and may pray without ceasing to God, to grant this nation repentance and forgiveness of the sin of slavery.[17]

History illustrates that the words of these two women, and many other abolitionists, were not entirely or immediately persuasive in the United States. Former slaves and Whites alike, people such as Harriet Beecher Stowe, Frederick Douglass, Sojourner Truth, Lucretia Mott, David Walker, and Harriet Tubman, invested their very lives in the committed work of freeing slaves in the southern United States and in places north as well. It would be a generation after the Grimké sisters released their pamphlets before slaves were emancipated, and generations more before basic rights would be recognized for those once enslaved. The argument could be made successfully today that people of conscience continue to struggle with such recognitions. The success of the abolitionists, however, cannot be measured by the comprehensiveness or speed of legislation. Their success is measured in faithfulness to the cause of stirring the conscience of a nation whose founding doctrines professed belief in God-given rights. Their success is measured in being faithful to God's Word and willing to be challenged by a deeper understanding of being made in God's image.

It should not be lost on us that while much has changed over the centuries with regard to Christians and the practice of slavery, much has remained the same. We still must ask ourselves if we see in others the very image of God that we wish to protect in ourselves. The treatment of human beings as commodities or possessions has not been erased across the globe. And while churches in our time do not usually condone slavery, we sometimes do turn a blind eye to practices and beliefs that continue to diminish the human person. It is critical to focus on our own spiritual growth, but if, at the same time, we ignore the systems and structures of oppression, we do so at our own peril.

While traditional forms of slavery have been outlawed in the United States and in most countries around the globe, we still detect its stench in human trafficking which involves forced labor, debt bondage, and sex trafficking. Governmental and social agencies estimate that this more recent form of slavery involves twenty-seven million adults and thirteen million children as victims around the globe. The numbers are staggering, equivalent to the current population of the state of California, and larger than the populations of Canada or Poland. And just to be clear, each number represents a human being, someone's daughter or son, someone's sister or brother.

Countries that rank highest as destinations for trafficked persons include Belgium, Germany, Greece, Israel, Italy, Japan, the Netherlands, Turkey and the United States, with the victims of trafficking coming most from Belarus, the Republic of Moldova, the Russian Federation, Ukraine, Albania, Bulgaria, Lithuania, Romania, China, Thailand, and Nigeria.[18] Clearly, slavery in every form has not disappeared, and people of faith are still challenged to uphold the golden rule.

The Golden Rule and a Parable of Judgment

In the Gospel of Matthew, the teaching role of Jesus is highlighted through collections of teachings scattered throughout the story line. It is as if Jesus is taking his followers through a training course, affirming what has been given by God in Judaism and then encouraging a fresh understanding of what it means to be faithful. As his public ministry progresses, Jesus' expectations become more and more evident until we arrive at a now familiar judgment scene, a scene that drives home the implications of loving God and neighbor, and the consequences of ignoring the golden rule. Surely the application to the practice of slavery is evident.

In Matthew 25:31-46, Jesus paints a picture of all the nations of the world assembling before the Son of Man. They are separated as a shepherd would sort through a flock of sheep and goats. The sheep will inherit the kingdom prepared for them from the foundation of the world, while the goats will be accursed and suffer eternal fire. The fate of each group (symbolized by sheep and goats) is determined by their own behavior. Have they embraced or rejected the deepest meaning of loving God and neighbor?

What does it look like to live according to the golden rule (treating others as ourselves)? And in what practical ways does a Christian extend love to one's neighbor and in the process love God as well? The parable in Matthew 25 is clear:

'For I was hungry and you gave me food, I was thirsty and you gave me something to drink, I was a stranger and you welcomed me, I was naked and you gave me clothing, I was sick and you took care of me, I was in prison and you visited me.' Then the righteous will answer him, 'Lord, when was it that we saw you hungry and gave you food, or thirsty and gave you something to drink? And when was it that we saw you a stranger and welcomed you, or naked and gave you clothing? And when was it that we saw you sick or in prison and visited you?' And the king will answer them, 'Truly I tell you, just as you did it to one of the least of these who are members of my family, you did it to me.' (Matthew 25:35-40)

There is no question that anyone held in slavery, in a situation of forced labor, is among the "least" of God's creatures. And just in case the argument begins that there were benevolent slave owners, those who treated their slaves more humanely, what can justify owning another person? Even as far back as Leviticus (19:34), God's intention is clear, even if God's people have taken centuries to absorb it: "The alien who lives with you shall be to you as the citizen among you, and you shall love the alien as yourself; for you were aliens in the land of Egypt: I am the LORD your God." Bit by bit, reading the Bible in the larger context of how God continually reveals himself and the meaning of his law, the culture that supports slavery is dismantled.

Setting the Captives Free

It is not a stretch to imagine how encouraged slaves would be by the mission of Jesus, or how that same mission emboldened the American abolitionists. And perhaps no passage better captures the essence of Jesus' mission than the scene described by Luke from the hometown of Jesus (see Luke 4:16-19). The Gospel writer describes Jesus going to synagogue as was his custom on the Sabbath. There, he was given the scroll of the prophet Isaiah to read to the assembly:

> "The Spirit of the Lord is upon me, / because he has anointed me / to bring good news to the poor. / He has sent me to proclaim / release to the captives / and recovery of sight to the blind, / to let the oppressed go free, / to proclaim the year of the Lord's favor" (Luke 4:18-19).

Now the proclamation of Isaiah's words would not have been unusual. Jewish synagogue-goers were quite accustomed to hearing the words of the prophets on a regular basis. But the text from Luke tells us two things that make this reading take on a new power in their midst, and for us. First, the eyes of all "were fixed on him," and second, Jesus announced that the ancient words were activated ("Today this scripture has been fulfilled in your hearing"; Luke 4:20-21). There is a sense that the authority of Jesus is made evident. Was it in his voice? In his stature? In a mix of confidence and humility?

In Luke's version of the events leading up to this moment in Nazareth, Jesus has just come out of the desert, having been tempted to satisfy human needs for food, power, and glory. Jesus met each temptation by quoting from the sacred writings of his tradition. His best defense against Satan was his grasp of the word of God, his immersion in its meaning and his commitment to the will of God revealed in those words. Perhaps it was that conviction about the revelation of God's will that made the words of Isaiah come alive when Jesus returned to his routine of going to synagogue after a forty-day desert retreat. His mission had begun and it was apparent that it would be a God-driven mission of liberation.

The content of Jesus' mission is simple but certainly not easy. His words and deeds would unsettle those who were comfortable with the power structure that was already in place. Some religious leaders at the time of Jesus were singled out for neglecting their duties in favor of guarding their positions. Jesus challenged scholars of the law and guardians of the Temple to know the heart of the law and place it at the center of their roles. Some of them found in Jesus a pest at best and an adversary at worst.

However, the anointing of Jesus is good news for the impoverished, for those held captive by disease or oppression. Just imagine the breath of hope that the poor would have felt in simply being the apple of Jesus' eye, and the object of his care and concern. Imagine the lepers who were healed and no longer exiled from their communities, the blind and deaf whose sight and hearing stood in contrast to the blind and deaf stubbornness of those opposed to Jesus. And then imagine how the words of Isaiah on the lips of Jesus echoed through the centuries and fell on the ears of people held in bondage on plantations and in manor houses in the United States or the West Indies or in Europe. Were slave owners using the words of Scripture to their benefit only? And were the clergy who were supportive of slavery measuring out God's mercy, stingily refusing to share it with the poor right under their noses?

How we hear and receive a proclamation of liberation is certainly tied to our position in a system of oppression, whether or not we are aware of it. At the time of Jesus, the assembly in Nazareth's synagogue was said to be "amazed" at his words, perhaps hopeful that they would be the beneficiaries of God's graciousness. However, just a few short verses later, after hearing Jesus offer an example of how God healed a non-Israelite in former times, the tide turned to fury.

It is one thing to believe in God's gracious mercy in theory, but quite another when God's mercy is extended to those deemed unworthy by cultural standards. The mission of Jesus, clear as it is, challenges the very foundation of slavery.

Treating Others as Ourselves

Christians are not the only ones whose teaching promotes human dignity and just treatment. Almost every world religious tradition professes some version of what we have come to call the golden rule, or the rule of reciprocity. Basically, we are to treat others as we would like to be treated. A few examples will illustrate this common shared belief:

- "If you seek justice, choose for others what you would choose for yourself." (Baha'i)

- "What you do not want done to yourself, do not unto others." (Confucianism)

- "Do naught to others which if done to thee would cause pain." (Hinduism)

- "No one of you is a believer until he loves for his brother what he loves for himself." (Islam)

- "We should . . . refrain from inflicting upon others such injury as would appear undesirable to us if inflicted upon ourselves." (Jainism)

- "What is hurtful to yourself, do not do to our fellow man." (Judaism)

- "To those who are good to me, I am also good; and to those who are not good to me, I am also good. And thus all get to be good." (Taoism)[19]

We cited earlier the golden rule found in Matthew's Gospel. Not only is this maxim a wisdom shared with other belief systems throughout history, for Christians it is the natural consequence of believing that each human person is made in God's image and likeness. Over time, as Christianity has matured and its adherents allow themselves to be shaped by the fullness of biblical testimony, it becomes clear that slavery flies in the face of the biblical tradition.

For Reflection:

- Is it possible that while slavery was common in biblical times, the principles to dismantle it were there all along? What factors might have prevented believers in the Judeo-Christian tradition from recognizing the rights and dignity of aliens, slaves, and others who were the least among them?

- In your faith community or parish, what are the avenues for staying informed about issues surrounding human dignity? How do you make sure that the biblical tradition is in dialogue with the real world we live in?

Chapter Six

All God's Children

Just around the corner from the building where I lived in graduate school was a beautiful gothic-inspired campus. Though not my own college, it was part of the consortium of schools that made up the Toronto School of Theology. Carved into the stone above the doors of their ivy-covered library was a snippet from chapter eight of John's Gospel: "The truth shall set you free." I loved to study there with its gorgeous stained-glass windows, polished wood floors, and softly lit tables. I suppose I felt I was immersing myself in the long tradition of learning and pondering deep things, and maybe even felt a kind of longing for something that I believe academia has always been at its core—a search for truth.

Little did I know then how profound the words of John would be as populations of the world cast about searching for truth and fighting for freedom. What might easily be a purely academic pursuit is, in fact, a search to understand what it means to be fully alive. To be set free, to be acknowledged as a human being made in the image of God, is the deep desire of anyone in bondage, whatever that bondage may be. While the Gospel of John 8:32 does not speak of the truth that sets free in the context of modern slavery, it nonetheless rings true to the situation of slavery. The Scriptures provide the truth about our God-given identity that becomes the basis for freedom.

Self-Understanding

An often-favored passage from Scripture is found in Jeremiah 1:5, "Before I formed you in the womb I knew you, / and before you were born I consecrated you." Jeremiah is describing his calling as God's prophet, and records the words from God that strengthened him for the hard task ahead. Over the centuries, this awareness of God's intention in creating Jeremiah has rightfully been applied to our own lives and callings. When we have an understanding that our very creation is God's initiative, and is filled with divine purpose and intention, we come to understand ourselves as worthy and worthwhile. Imagine such a realization in the life of those who are bought, beaten, and belittled.

Such a sense of having been shaped and chosen by God, of being children of God, permeates the Bible's pages. In the Old Testament in particular, God's people are reminded that they belong to God as to a parent. Moses was sent to Pharaoh to demand release of the Hebrew people, God's "firstborn" (Exodus 4:22). The laws spelled out in the Torah flow from an awareness that these former slaves are "children of the LORD" (Deuteronomy 14:1). God loved Israel like a father loves his own child (Hosea 11:1; Wisdom 18:13).

The biblical stories of individuals also communicate their sense of having been made and sent by God. Abraham, Isaac, Jacob, Moses, Israel's kings and prophets, Peter, Paul and Barnabas are assured in various ways that they are precious in the sight of God, cared for and commissioned for God's purposes. And while it is true that many of these individual stories are told through the experience of men, we can also point to Sarah and Hagar, Miriam, Judith, and Esther, Mary, Mary Magdalene, and more.

In fact, there are wonderful elements to familiar stories that are often overlooked. One such example is found in the story of Sarah and Hagar (Genesis 16–18, 21:1-20). Given that Hagar was a foreign slave-girl to Sarah, and concubine to Abraham, the episode is worth considering in this exploration of slavery and freedom. In broad strokes, the biblical story describes how Abraham came to have descendants. God promised Abraham that his progeny would be as numerous as the stars or the dust of the earth or the grains of sand (Genesis 12:1-3; 13:14-16; 15:1-6; 22:17), and yet his wife Sarah had borne no children and was past her childbearing years.

The account that unfolds in Genesis tells us that Sarah employed a common, culturally acceptable practice at the time. She offered her slave to Abraham to produce the heir that God had promised, saying, "I will obtain children by her" (Genesis 16:2). We are given no indication that Hagar consented to this arrangement. Hagar was property to be shared, and the child would be credited to Sarah. The text tells us that once pregnant, Hagar felt contempt for

Sarah but the reader cannot help but wonder if it might have been the other way around. Sarah first shifted blame for the mess to Abraham, and eventually so mistreated her pregnant slave that Hagar ran into the wilderness where an angel of God appeared to Hagar in her misery and told her to return and submit to Sarah. That piece of instruction probably offends our modern sensibilities. We struggle along with Hagar to make sense of such a command.

And this is where we might miss a significant piece of the story. "The angel of the LORD also said to her, 'I will so greatly multiply your offspring that they cannot be counted for multitude'" (Genesis 16:10). Like the patriarch Abraham, this slave woman receives a promise from God that her descendants will be too numerous to count. In spite of her lowly status, and in the midst of her inability to control her own fate, she is on a par with Abraham in terms of coming to understand God's care for her in the messy circumstances of her life. Later, when Sarah has miraculously borne her own son and the two boys are growing up together, Hagar again becomes the object of Sarah's wrath and jealousy. Once more, God gives the assurance that Ishmael, on the verge of starving with his mother in the desert, will become a great nation.

In the midst of her slavery, Hagar discovers her own God-given dignity. It is a story that could have been tucked away and lost to generations who revere the Bible. The beauty of it is found not so much in its historical accuracy; its point was to try to give some explanation for the much later historical rifts that surfaced in the region. Its beauty, rather, is found in the very fact that it is included in the sacred text of Israel, hinting at the wideness of God's mercy and the depth of God's care for all sons and daughters, slave or free.

The story of Hagar may not be repeated in its details in every corner of the world. However, the discovery and affirmation of her own worth is repeated in all kinds of places where slavery and its descendent, racism, continue to appear. One example comes to mind. The nine Black students who were the first to integrate Central High School in 1957 in Little Rock, Arkansas, endured all kinds of threats to their lives simply because they were Black and would be attending classes alongside White students. Daisy Gaston Bates, the local president of the National Association for the Advancement of Colored People (NAACP), had chosen bright students who would voluntarily help to integrate the school system and she stood with them and their parents throughout their trials. What followed was bedlam, involving the Arkansas National Guard who were ordered by the governor to block the students from entering the school, the United States Army who eventually escorted the students inside, scores of reporters, and riled up parents and students. And of course the chaos and hostility did not end there.

The Little Rock Nine, as they came to be known, must have discovered even in the midst of deep-rooted racism that they were worthy and they were capable. Their individual achievements serve as a testament: an employee in the United States Department of the Interior, another in the United States Department of Labor, a journalist and

educator, an army veteran, an aerospace research techni-
cian, a property broker, a probation officer, and a psycholo-
gist. In 1999, forty-two years after their own wilderness
experience in the halls of a high school, they were each
awarded the Congressional Gold Medal.[20]

Many years later, one of the nine, Melba Pattillo Beals,
reflected on her experience in 1957:

> Every day, white students hit, kicked and spit on
> me. When I went to the bathroom, they tossed
> burning strips of paper over the stall. I walked
> the halls in constant fear. When I complained
> to Dr. Martin Luther King, Jr., about the treat-
> ment we received each day, he said, "Don't be
> selfish, Melba. You are doing this for generations
> yet unborn." He changed the direction of my
> commitment. "You can always call on the Lord,"
> Grandma told me. "He's as close as your skin."[21]

After a tumultuous year at Central High School, and
another year studying at home while Little Rock schools
were closed because of integration, Melba spent her senior
year with a family in California who took her in as one
of their own. It was a White family, Quakers who were
actively involved with the NAACP; yet another experience
of feeling like an outsider, at least at first. She writes about
struggling to determine where she belonged:

> Finally, I understood. My true home wasn't a
> particular place or even with particular people.

It was with God. He gave me the vision to see beyond what segregated society dictated. He had given me the courage to raise my hand to enter Central. He would keep giving me the strength and support I needed to follow my own path.[22]

Spirit of Slavery vs. Spirit of Adoption

In the New Testament, Paul picks up the thread of God's special care and reminds the followers of Jesus that we too are God's family: "For all who are led by the Spirit of God are children of God. For you did not receive a spirit of slavery to fall back into fear, but you have received a spirit of adoption. . . . " (Romans 8:14-15). Most scholars would agree that the fear Paul speaks of is fear of death, and that with the resurrection of Jesus, that fear is put to rest. But what are we to make of the spirit of slavery and the spirit of adoption? This is a theme echoed in Galatians 4:7, which reads, "So you are no longer a slave but a child, and if a child then also an heir, through God."

We've seen that slavery was an ongoing institution throughout biblical history. And, we might be right in presuming that much of the slavery we hear about in Scripture is not necessarily tied to skin color or ethnicity, but is wed to a person's financial status—the poor being in the position of slaves and the wealthy in the position of owning slaves. While adoption was fairly uncommon among Jews at the time of Paul, it was not completely unheard of in Jewish tradition. Adoption in some form could have occurred in the case of Ishmael, the son of Hagar who acted as a surrogate mother for Sarah and Abraham. We know that Pharaoh's daughter famously rescued baby Moses from the reeds of the river and raised him as a son in her household (Exodus 2:10). Family members sometimes took in orphaned relatives, as was the case with Esther and Mordacai (Esther 2:7) and with Ephraim and Manasseh who were adopted by Jacob (Genesis 48:5-6). Additionally, adoption was a familiar part of the Greco-Roman world where the gospel was spreading, and carried the weight of legal inheritance. So, Paul was using somewhat familiar real-world institutions, slavery and adoption, to speak of a spiritual reality.

The spirit of slavery that Paul speaks of in Galatians, and repeats in his letter to the church in Rome, is generally understood as slavery to sin. Of course, sin can be understood as sinful acts that violate the laws of God. More critically, sin is participating in the worldly or cultural attitudes that put us at odds with the great commands to love God and neighbor, and the command to treat others as we would ourselves. As we've already seen, the culturally accepted practice of actual slavery puts a believer more in line with the surrounding culture than with the internal life God gives to each person.

Paul offers God's alternative to the spirit of slavery when he speaks of the spirit of adoption, affirming that we belong to God: "We are children of God, and if children, then heirs, heirs of God and joint heirs with Christ—if, in fact, we suffer with him so that we may also be glorified with him" (Romans 8:16b-17). In the ancient Jewish and Greco-Roman world where Christianity was born and first flourished, being adopted as a son, in particular, made one an heir. Paul is not suggesting that only males are adopted as siblings of Jesus but that all believers have the status that was once reserved only for sons. And just as Jesus already has his inheritance—eternal life and love with God—we are entering into our inheritance which is the glory destined for us even through suffering. This truth is not just a confirmation of our own status as believers but a call to evangelize so that all people share in this reality.

The Scriptures invite us to imagine a world where all kinds of slavery are abolished as we recognize our common humanity and our common God-given dignity. Plantation slavery, human trafficking, addictions of various kinds—all are enabled by a false sense of self where either we treat others as unworthy, or feel it ourselves. The good news of Jesus is that we are members of one family and there are no favorites. Paul offers a real-world example of this in his brief but challenging appeal to Philemon.

Onesimus, a Slave or a Brother?

The Letter to Philemon is perhaps the most perplexing New Testament story that demands our attention in terms of slavery. At the heart of this letter is the reality of slavery, again not directly condemned but perhaps transformed. Written by Paul during an imprisonment, possibly his final imprisonment in Rome, the letter addresses a household of believers: "To Philemon our dear friend and co-worker, to Apphia our sister, to Archippus our fellow soldier, and to the church in your house" (Philemon 1-2). The usual greetings of grace and remembrance open the letter, and then Paul gets right to the point. A slave who escaped Philemon's household has been with Paul, has been converted by Paul, and is being sent back to Philemon.

Onesimus is not being returned for a beating, which was Philemon's right in punishing a runaway slave. Rather, Onesimus the slave is being returned as Onesimus the fellow Christian. Philemon, the slave owner, is being given the opportunity to experience his slave as a brother in Christ. Paul writes:

> I wanted to keep him with me, so that he might be of service to me in your place during my imprisonment for the gospel; but I preferred to do nothing without your consent, in order that your good deed might be voluntary and not something forced. Perhaps this is the reason he was separated from you for a while, so that you might have him back forever, no longer as a slave but more than a slave, a beloved brother—especially to me but how much more to you, both in the flesh and in the Lord. (Philemon 13-16)

Throughout this brief letter, it is obvious that Paul is invoking Philemon's higher calling, his identity in Christ, hoping to convince this slave owner that baptism has transformed the slave/master relationship. Furthermore, Paul calls upon Philemon's affection (verse 9), asks him to show the love Paul has experienced to Onesimus, offers to pay whatever damages Onesimus has accrued (verse 18), and then reminds Philemon of his own debt to Paul (verse 19). It appears to be a warm appeal, with a bit of a guilt trip thrown in for good measure!

We have no way of knowing with certainty how Paul's letter to Philemon was received. Did he punish Onesimus, begrudgingly welcome him, or forge a new relationship? Did Onesimus stay with Philemon and his family? Did he grow into an identity informed by slavery but not limited to its boundaries? I'd like to think that one step at a time, one situation at a time, Christianity began the task of walking toward freedom that was not only spiritual but physical. History shows, however, that it has been a very slow journey.

In previous public letters that Paul wrote to various communities, he teaches that Christianity dissolves the differences that at one time defined relationships in the Greco-Roman world (and sometimes does so still). It was not an accomplished reality in Paul's time, nor is it still, but allowing the truth of our identity in Christ to shape us also forces us to move toward greater accountability. The core Christian value that we are all God's children asks us to examine our conscience individually and collectively, to be willing to tear down walls that separate us and build relationships that not only will sustain us but will transform our world. Paul holds out this ideal:

In Christ Jesus you are all children of God
through faith. As many of you as were baptized
into Christ have clothed yourselves with Christ.
There is no longer Jew or Greek, there is no longer
slave or free, there is no longer male and female;
for all of you are one in Christ Jesus. (Galatians
3:26-28)

For just as the body is one and has many members,
and all the members of the body, though many,
are one body, so it is with Christ. For in the one
Spirit we were all baptized into one body—Jews
or Greeks, slaves or free—and we were all made
to drink of one Spirit. (1 Corinthians 12:12-13)

The story of Onesimus and Philemon may cause us to
bemoan the missed opportunity to condemn slavery as an
institution, but consider that the New Testament reflects
a period of time when the return of Christ was imminent.
There was an immediacy to the message of the apostles and
others who were doing the work of evangelization. While
that does not excuse ignoring institutional change, it does
serve as a reminder that the work of the gospel is always
unfolding in the midst of a world where injustice bubbles
up and commands our attention and our constant commitment to bring God's justice and mercy.

For Reflection:

- What experiences have helped you to see yourself as a child of God, worthy of God's care and attention?

- The biblical stories of Hagar and Onesimus, and more contemporary experiences like that of the Little Rock Nine, invite us to consider our own loyalties and prejudgments. What pieces of these stories can you relate to?

Chapter Seven

From Dreams to Reality

In August of 1963, Martin Luther King Jr., stood on the steps of the Lincoln Memorial in the nation's capital and delivered one of the most famous and often quoted speeches in American history. Known simply as the "I have a dream" speech, King fanned the flames of racial reform and those flames have not and will not be extinguished. Listeners then and now cannot help but be struck by the power of his call for racial equality through peaceful means. He spoke with clarity in describing the racial injustice that had flowed since the founding of this country, and with a real and powerful sense of hope for what can be as history continues to unfold.

The "I have a dream" speech made ample use of Scripture. Dr. King himself was shaped by the biblical tradition, and he understood its power to evoke in the human spirit the desire for truth and the means to pursue it. Speaking of the Emancipation Proclamation that led to freedom for slaves in America in the nineteenth century, he said, "It came as a joyous daybreak to end the long night of their captivity."[23] King is evoking the Hebrew emancipation from slavery in Egypt, and the later freedom from captivity in Babylon. He is joining the fight for freedom in every age to the fight for freedom in ancient times.

Later in his speech, as he painted a picture of a future America where equality is realized, King demonstrated his understanding of God's reign. His words echo those of John the Baptist in the Gospels (see Matthew 3:1-3; Mark 1:2-4; Luke 3:4-6; John 1:23), who echoed the ancient words of an earlier prophet (see Isaiah 40:3-5). King declared: "I have a dream that one day every valley shall be exalted, every hill and mountain shall be made low, the rough places will be made plain, and the crooked places will be made straight, and the glory of the Lord shall be revealed, and all flesh shall see it together." [24]

The coming of Jesus has to impact the world of sin, oppression and despair. It has to bring hope for the hopeless in real circumstances. Martin Luther King, and many others in the push for civil rights, knew this to be true. And so, King envisioned a world where children of slaves and slave owners will share a common table, where places of racial injustice will become oases of freedom, and where people will be judged by character and not by skin color.

Most contemporary civil rights leaders did not personally experience physical slavery but they recognize, and help us to do so as well, that slavery is planted with the seeds of perceived inequality. Economies built on slavery in ancient times, or even in today's world, cannot exist without the "haves" in a society feeling a false sense of superiority over the "have-nots." Unfortunately, in societies around the world, these divisions fall not only along economic lines but along racial and ethnic lines. Freedom, then, becomes liberation from physical bondage, as well as liberation from stereotypes and patterns of thinking and acting that diminish the human person.

Slaves, Obey Your Masters

So far, it seems that we have been on a path through Scripture that bit by bit dismantles the underpinnings of slavery, and therefore the foundations of racism and classism. We acknowledge that slavery exists throughout the biblical period, and that there is no outright condemnation of the practice, but at the same time we have seen the case building for unity that, in fact, cannot exist without equality. There are still puzzling passages that need our attention.

One such passage was referenced in our first chapter. In his letter to the Ephesians (6:5-9), Paul writes:

> Slaves, obey your earthly masters with fear and trembling, in singleness of heart, as you obey Christ; not only while being watched, and in order to please them, but as slaves of Christ, doing the will of God from the heart. Render service with enthusiasm, as to the Lord and not to men and women, knowing that whatever good we do, we will receive the same again from the Lord, whether we are slaves or free. And, masters, do the same to them. Stop threatening them, for

you know that both of you have the same Master in heaven, and with him there is no partiality.

The first verse of this passage provided a tool misused by Christian slave masters to keep their unpaid and abused laborers in line. Slave owners could believe themselves filling the role of Christ in the lives of their slaves! But they could believe that only by ignoring the immediate context of Paul's letter, and by disregarding the broader context of Scripture and Christian tradition.

Paul's letter to the Ephesians was written during the last third of the first century to promote the unity of the church. Beginning in Ephesians 4:25, Paul turns his attention from a beautiful theology of unity in Christ to the practical applications of that unity in communities of faith. Hearers and readers are urged to live in such a way that light comes pouring in through their communities. There are reminders about honest and uplifting speech, and avoiding greed and other sins that disrupt community life. Paul then outlines what is sometimes called a "household code." In these verses (Ephesians 5:21–6:9), he proposes what he considers appropriate relationships between spouses, between children and parents, and then between slaves and masters.

Numerous first-century writings in the Greco-Roman world include some form of a household code as a way to promote order. In the New Testament, in addition to Ephesians, there are several other sets of household codes (see Colossians 3:18–4:1; 1 Timothy 2:1-15; Titus 2:1-10; 1 Peter 2:11–3:7). These biblical household codes reflect a time in early Christianity when communities of faith were eager to demonstrate that they would not be disruptive to the cultural and legal norms of the Roman Empire, even to the point of accepting the economy provided by slavery.

Household codes in New Testament letters also reflect a time in early Christianity when many waited with eager expectation for the second coming of Christ, not as some far-off reality but as something just around the corner (see Titus 2:13). When Paul tells slaves to obey their masters (Ephesians 6:5-9; Colossians 3:22), remember also that he instructs believers generally to stay in the state in which they find themselves as they await Christ's coming (see 1 Corinthians 7). Single people are to remain single, married couples remain married even if one's spouse does not profess Christianity, circumcised or uncircumcised also are to remain as they are. It is in this context that slaves are instructed to obey their masters, with the reminder to "render service with enthusiasm, as to the Lord and not to men and women, knowing that whatever good we do, we will receive the same again from the Lord, whether we are slaves or free" (Ephesians 6:7-8).

We read the household codes of Ephesians and Colossians in our current context and surely think them out of sync with reality. However, there is a bit of movement in the direction of freedom and equality, at least for that time and place. While not overturning the staid roles of women and slaves, for example, these codes do propose a relational understanding of these roles that is quite different from the secular codes of the time. Women, children, and slaves were definitely seen as lesser in importance than free males. These groups were regarded as property and were, therefore, more vulnerable to the abuse of power. It is a step in a new direction when Paul urges husbands and wives to be subordinate to one another, and commands husbands to love their wives as Christ loves the church. It is a step in a new direction to urge parents not to anger their children (we could understand that as advice not to abuse their children). It is a step in a new direction to tell slave masters to stop threatening their slaves but, instead, to realize God shows no partiality.

All that being said, if we were the ones enslaved, this trajectory might be small comfort. And given how rampant slavery was in the first Christian century, it is likely that most of the community members Paul addressed were slaves or would have been at some time in their lives. The gospel message is that in Christ all are set free, regardless of one's state in life. It is hard to know if slaves dared hope to believe that freedom from slavery would be both physical and spiritual.

Slaves of Christ

As we have already seen, Paul is no stranger to the institution of slavery, and apparently he is no fan of it in the Christian community as it tends to erode the unity that the church is called to embrace. His theology revolves around the accomplishments of Christ who dissolves all divisions.

Paul has a deep appreciation for the necessity of the cross to accomplish salvation for all, and he takes seriously the role of the cross in every Christian life, including his own.

The hymn we find in Philippians 2 beautifully expresses the pattern of descent and exaltation that Paul sees, and invites us to imitate, in the life of Christ:

> Let the same mind be in you that was in Christ
> Jesus,
> who, though he was in the form of God,
> did not regard equality with God
> as something to be exploited,
> but emptied himself,
> taking the form of a slave,
> being born in human likeness.
> And being found in human form,
> he humbled himself
> and became obedient to the point of death—
> even death on a cross.
> Therefore God also highly exalted him
> and gave him the name
> that is above every name,
> so that at the name of Jesus
> every knee should bend,
> in heaven and on earth and under the earth,
> and every tongue should confess
> that Jesus Christ is Lord,
> to the glory of God the Father.
> (Philippians 2:5-11)

Paul turns the reality of slavery on its head as he describes the humility of Christ in verse 7, saying he "emptied himself, / taking the form of a slave, / being born in human likeness." Paul understood that the incarnation of Jesus was the epitome of surrendering to the will of God, and so he used the reality of slavery to describe the submission of Jesus to the will of the Father. In what might be the boldest of ironies, the cross, a symbol of hate and destruction and death, became in Christianity the symbol of love and restoration and life. This is not to say that Christianity embraces execution; quite the opposite. We see in this tool of punishment that God can bring redemption even through the worst of circumstances. Perhaps it is better to understand it as holding the two opposite realities in tension: the cross is cruel and deadly as well as the ultimate avenue to eternal life. Could the same sense of holding opposites be true of slavery?

In several passages in letters attributed to Paul, he describes himself as a slave of Christ Jesus. The New Revised Standard Version prefers "servant" to translate the Greek word *doulos*, which softens the effect. However, the word itself does indeed mean "slave" and there is little doubt that this was what Paul meant to say.

Imagine the people in those communities who received his letters, hearing an elder read the letter's greeting aloud: "Paul and Timothy, slaves of Christ Jesus . . . " (Philippians 1:1), or "Paul, a slave of Jesus Christ, called to be an apostle, set apart for the gospel of God . . . " (Romans 1:1). If many of his original hearers were slaves themselves, how would they have heard these words?

- Would they have heard Paul saying that he too is a slave but that his master is the Messiah, the Christ?

- Was he saying that slavery is nothing to be ashamed of, but who the master is matters?

- If some in the community were slaveholders, was Paul shaming them by attesting to the superiority of his master?

Further, do slaves in the modern world, centuries later, hear Paul's self-description differently still? Was he saying that he is walking with them, putting on the yoke of slavery so that he knows their suffering and they will know his glory?

In one of his letters to the church in Corinth, when Paul speaks of himself and Apollos, he uses the Greek word, *hyperetes* for "servant." He says to the church, "Think of us in this way, as servants of Christ and stewards of God's mysteries" (1 Corinthians 4:1). Interestingly, here it is not the word for servant that catches our attention but another term. The word translated as "steward" (Greek, *oikonomos*) in this passage can also refer to a slave, in this case a domestic slave who might have some supervisory role over other household slaves. Paul seems to be saying that he and Apollos are slaves of Christ and that they have responsibilities to minister not in their own name but in the name of and with the trust of God. They feel the obligation to demonstrate their devotion to God in living as Christ did, humble and obedient to God's will, and with responsibility for others in their care.

In the course of these descriptions we get the sense that Paul is elevating the status of slaves, not in their own right, but in their devotion to God, whatever their circumstances. Writing to the church in Corinth, Paul says, "Whoever was called in the Lord as a slave is a freed person belonging to the Lord, just as whoever was free when called is a slave of Christ" (1 Corinthians 7:22). One's dignity is not determined by social status or the lack of it, but by the freedom granted in Christ. Paul is not dismissive of the cruelty that accompanies slavery nor the realities of oppression that are condemned in the Exodus events and the words of the prophets from his own Jewish tradition. He acknowledges that God liberates all from oppression. However, Paul sees in the death and resurrection of Jesus an additional facet of freedom that is spiritual and demands self-sacrificing love, which he describes, ironically, as the kind of slavery that sets us free.

If you feel like you have been turning in circles, you are probably not alone. In the ancient world, slavery was a fact of life. Paul is saying to his audience that they have the ability to choose their ultimate master. Will their identity be forever wed to a human master who may or may not be honest or fair? Or will their identity be discovered in a complete devotion to Christ, who chose to liberate all bound by the slavery of sin? Paul says he chooses to serve Christ, to be his slave, to follow in the footsteps of one who became a slave on our behalf.

As a reminder, in the ancient world slavery was often a life that one submitted to in order to pay off debts. Paul reminds his audience in every age, "You were bought with a price; do not become slaves of human masters" (1 Corinthians 7:23). The ultimate debt we owe for our very lives has been paid by the cross of Christ. At the core of our being, we experience a spiritual freedom that cannot be bound no matter our circumstances.

Freedom for Service

In the early generations of the church, believers struggled with the role of the law of Moses in their communities. This is especially true because the earliest believers were Jews who accepted that Jesus was the Messiah, and with Jesus came a renewed understanding of the spirit of the law. As the initial followers of Jesus were joined by Gentiles, many of whom were unfamiliar with the law of Moses, Paul and other leaders struggled to express the unity demanded of the circumcised (Jews) and the uncircumcised (Gentiles). At the heart of this post-resurrection reality is the experience of freedom.

Let's return to a Gospel account. Following the often quoted "the truth will make you free" passage in John 8, Jesus' contemporary Jewish listeners protest his implication that they are bound in some way; they are not slaves and have never been. Interestingly, they seem to have set aside the experience of their ancestors' slavery in Egypt. Some would also say that Jews at the time of Jesus and his immediate followers, their country dominated by Roman occupiers, were living in a somewhat enslaved situation once again. But Jesus is more interested in a different form of slavery, and responds: "Very truly, I tell you, everyone who commits sin is a slave to sin. The slave does not have a permanent place in the household; the son has a place there forever. So if the Son makes you free, you will be free indeed" (John 8:34-36). Throughout John's Gospel, Jesus tells his listeners that beyond knowledge of the law, there is the experience of knowing God intimately through Jesus, the Son of God (John 1:14; 4:23-26; 14:6-7). This is the root of the spiritual freedom that defines Christians, and what Paul speaks about in his letters. This is why he can say that whether slave or not, all are free.

Further, the freedom that Christians experience is not simply a "freedom from" but is also a "freedom for." Paul expresses this clearly in his letter to the church in Galatia, reminding them, and centuries later reminding us, that we are to stand firm in freedom and not submit again to the yoke of slavery. Again, this is the yoke of sinfulness, the ever-present pull against the freedom we know in Christ: "For you were called to freedom, brothers and sisters; only do not use your freedom as an opportunity for self-indulgence, but through love become slaves to one another. For the whole law is summed up in a single commandment, 'You shall love your neighbor as yourself'" (Galatians 5:13-14).

We have arrived back at the golden rule. And we have discovered again that slavery can be turned on its ear. To "become slaves to one another" is not to say that we are chained against our wills. Rather, in a strange twist, laying down our lives in mutual service will be a sign of our freedom.

For Reflection:

- Why do you suppose is it sometimes easier to apply Jesus' teachings to spiritual bondage and freedom than to physical bondage and freedom?

- How has the experience of service become an affirmation of freedom in your life? In the lives of others you admire?

Chapter Eight

Free at Last

Early in my adult life I was a classroom teacher, first in a grade school and later in a high school. One of the lessons I learned quite quickly is that students are sometimes marked by their reputation, or that of a sibling, long before they enter the next grade. Actually, I understood this dynamic even from my own days as a student. A child perceived as a troublemaker by one teacher could be seen as inventive by another, unless the child is painted as a problem student and the perception gets passed on year after year. Siblings might have difficulty making their own mark, based on their own merits—shaking off the bad reputation of a sister or brother on the one hand, or living up to the stellar achievements of an older sibling. These experiences hold power in their ability to shape our perceptions of the world.

Another lesson that I have learned in the course of living is the power of words to shape our external behavior and our internal worlds. The athlete who is perceived as all brawn and no brain, who is told that he or she can only excel in a sports arena, may not explore other possibilities. On the other hand, that same athlete might be challenged to translate the leadership and critical thinking skills learned on the field or court of play to shape an entirely different future. A child who hears "you're stupid," "you'll amount to nothing," and "you're a loser" will begin to believe it is true, while a child who hears the opposite will begin to believe that is true. The power of words is not a lesson in wishful or positive thinking. Words have power because they too help to shape perceptions, as well as encourage the development and use of skills, and affirm the dignity of the human person.

The examples I offer, while rather simple, speak to something much more profound when applied to the centuries of various forms of slavery around the world, and particularly in the United States. Think of the power of the collective experience of being held as property by another human being, of being perceived as "less than" even after being freed. Consider the power of language used to "master" a people for one's own purposes. What lingering messages take root and continue to spring up through the generations? And yet, there is hope that the seeds of liberation may yet blossom as they are planted deep within as well. In his book, *No Longer Slaves*, Brad R. Braxton, describes it this way:

> If an oppressor can shackle a people in chains and eradicate even the slightest remembrance of their former life of freedom and concomitantly assassinate their hope for future freedom, it may be possible to convince the oppressed that the chains around their wrists, ankles, and minds are natural. But if the oppressed people hide even the most minute reminiscence of freedom in

their hearts or have maintained even the smallest ability to imagine what freedom must be like, the chains for such people do not square existentially with their past or dreamt-for future.[25]

It is that hidden hope of freedom that must have carried slaves when their backs were strained as they worked land that would never be theirs and harvested crops that would feed others. It is that imagination for freedom that must have given them the courage to stand as they were beaten and abused. It is that hidden seed of freedom that reminds those enslaved in human trafficking today that they are worth far more than the treatment they receive would indicate. And that same seed of freedom is what allows those enslaved to addictive behaviors to eventually break out of the patterns that devalue them.

Those influenced by the breadth of the biblical tradition recognize that freedom, even in its tiniest seed form, is the result of God's presence and goodness. Those who preserved the narrative of salvation in oral and then in written form over the centuries experienced God as a liberator. They recognized that their own desire for true freedom was itself a reflection of the divine image implanted within them. Their testimony in the pages of our Bibles calls us to claim the freedom that is ours and to ensure that others know the profound depth of liberation that God desires for us. Perhaps that is why Martin Luther King Jr's proclamation in our own time still rings with such hope: "Free at last, Free at last. Thank God almighty, we are free at last."

Freedom from Fear

The psalms are the prayer book of God's people. Crafted during the time of Israel's monarchy and their later exile, the psalms reflect multiple images of God and what it means to faithfully trust in God. Perhaps the most familiar of these prayers is at its heart a testimony about God's presence in the midst of hardship, oppression, or evil: "Even though I walk through the darkest valley, / I will fear no evil, / for you are with me" (Psalm 23:4). An assurance of God's presence casts out fear.

Many of the psalms praise God for the Hebrew liberation from Egypt, and they continue to resonate with God's people beyond that period because they testify to God's desire to free us from all forms of captivity. Additionally, there are psalms that cry out to God for protection, demonstrating that even in times of fear and danger, we can trust God to hear us and give comfort and security.

The psalmist calls out to God, "O Most High, when I am afraid, / I put my trust in you. / In God, whose word I praise, / in God I trust; I am not afraid; / what can flesh do to me?" (Psalm 56:3–4). We might imagine that such confidence is as much about reassuring the psalmist as it is about praising God and invoking God's help. Words of confidence in God are a powerful antidote to fear. When we pray the psalms, from whatever situation threatens to bind us in fear, the words themselves remind us to trust God to deliver us.

Psalm 91 also can serve as an example of the freedom to be found in trusting God's care. This prayer extols us to experience the benefits of living in the shelter of the Most High and abiding in the shadow of the Almighty. This is a place of security and protection, which in turn becomes a place for deliverance from deadly pestilence, terrors of the night, and arrows that fly by day. In fact, the psalmist says, "Because you have made the LORD your refuge, / the Most High your dwelling place, / no evil shall befall you, / no scourge come near your tent" (Psalm 91:9-10). Angels are sent to protect God's people, saving them from even injuring themselves upon the stones.

When Jesus began his ministry with a time of fasting and prayer in the desert, the Gospels tell us that the devil tempted Jesus (Matthew 4:5-7; Luke 4:9-12). By quoting Psalm 91, the devil mocked the kind of trust that would rely on angels for protection. Jesus did not throw himself down from the heights in order to test God but stood his ground. Jesus' liberation from the devil's taunts flowed from in an inner certainty of how God was acting in him. There is no doubt that Jesus would have known the psalm in its entirety. He could have been allowing the words to roll around in his heart, hearing the final verses:

> Those who love me, I will deliver;
> I will protect those who know my name.
>
> When they call to me, I will answer them;
> I will be with them in trouble,
> I will rescue them and honor them.
> With long life I will satisfy them,
> and show them my salvation. (Psalm 91:14-16)

Fear of what may happen, and fear in the midst of what is happening, can rob us of living in the sure confidence that God is with us no matter the circumstances. It can also cripple our efforts to serve God's purposes in difficult situations. In Paul's second letter to Timothy, written to encourage the young evangelist, he writes, "I remind you to rekindle the gift of God that is within you through the laying on of my hands; for God did not give us a spirit of cowardice, but rather a spirit of power and of love and of self-discipline" (2 Timothy 1:6-7). In order for Timothy to take on the mantle of leadership, he needed words that were filled not simply with encouragement but with the deep truth that God would provide what he needed. In this case, Timothy needed freedom from a spirit of cowardice or fear.

There may not have been a better person to pass on that liberating message to Timothy than Paul. Even when chained and facing eventual death, Paul knew freedom. We can imagine him murmuring the various phrases of the psalms as he awaited trial, "I sought the LORD, and he answered me, / and delivered me from all my fears" (Psalm 34:4). He could express joy (Philippians 1:18-20), courage (Ephesians 6:19-20), and serenity (2 Timothy 4:6-8) as he continued to minister; lacking physical freedom, Paul was fully aware of his spiritual freedom.

Freedom from Worry and Anxiety

While fear can have a positive side in the form of making prudent decisions and avoiding real danger if possible, it has "cousins" in the form of worry and anxiety that have few real benefits. Wringing our hands and playing out in our minds scenarios of doom can have the effect of binding our hearts, preventing us from experiencing the freedom that God created in us and wills for us. Worry and anxiety rob us of hope, and hope is a precious seed that flowers into freedom.

Again, we can turn to the psalms to find the words that become our prayer no matter the type of anxiety we are experiencing. In Psalm 94, the psalmist prays a lament, calling on God to give the wicked their due. Many of us may feel real discomfort calling out to the "God of vengeance" as this psalmist does. It's probably not an image of God that we want to promote and yet, when feeling the weight of oppression or injustice against us or others, we do want God to act on our behalf and to squash evil in all its forms. As with most psalms of lament, there is a tone of "how long, O Lord" that is balanced with a calm assurance that God is worthy of our trust and will win out in the end. Single lines of Scripture can serve as a mantra of assurance and a prayerful reminder:

> When the cares of my heart are many, your consolations cheer my soul. (Psalm 94:19)

> But the LORD has become my stronghold, and my God the rock of my refuge. (Psalm 94:22)

Each of us can relate in some way to carrying the weight of "the cares of my heart," also translated as anxiety, and the desire for a just and sure resolution. There is comfort in knowing that we are not alone in our external situations or in our inner worlds.

Centuries later, the evangelists did their best to capture the powerful words of Jesus about freedom from worry and anxiety. Matthew and Luke each contain a version of Jesus' teaching: "Therefore I tell you, do not worry about your life, what you will eat or what you will drink, or about your body, what you will wear. Is not life more than food, and the body more than clothing" (Matthew 6:25; see also Luke 12:22-23). In these accounts, Jesus is teaching multitudes of people who no doubt are worried about their next meal and how to clothe their children. In his typical fashion, Jesus goes on to illustrate this by pointing to the birds of the air that do not have grain storage and the flowers of the field who are resplendent simply by blowing in the wind.

Surely Jesus is not saying that feeding and clothing one's family is unnecessary, or unworthy of attention. Try leaving it at that with a person struggling with addiction, or whose family is threatened with violence or poverty, or who lives in servitude to others against his will. Rather, Jesus seems to be addressing the issue of attachment, the way we humans tend to hold on to things, to plans, and to ideologies. These attachments are often at the root of our anxieties. St. Francis de Sales might say that Jesus was creating in us a sense of "holy detachment" or "holy indifference."[26] Those who are in the throes of physical slavery have little choice but to give up their attachments as their belongings are few if any, and their family members are ripped away from them. Those enslaved to addictions become detached from anything that does not feed that addiction. These detachments are forced and oppressive. Instead, Jesus is encouraging a detachment that is rooted in God's loving care: "But strive first for the kingdom of God and his righteousness, and all these things will be given to you as well" (Matthew 6:33).

Peter, another of Jesus' disciples, also addressed the issue of freedom from anxiety. His advice is a combination of assurance, discipline, and reward: "Cast all your anxiety on him, because he cares for you. Discipline yourselves, keep alert. Like a roaring lion your adversary the devil prowls around, looking for someone to devour. Resist him, steadfast in your faith, for you know that your brothers and sisters in all the world are undergoing the same kinds of suffering. And after you have suffered for a little while, the God of all grace, who has called you to his eternal glory in Christ, will himself restore, support, strengthen, and establish you" (1 Peter 5:7-10). The powerful assurance of the first line, "Cast all your anxiety on him, because he cares for you" is like that little seed of freedom we referred to earlier. Learning to trust in God sets us free from anxiety, and then allows for growth in discipline and endurance.

Setting our Hearts on Peace

Almost every time we read in Scripture words along the lines of "do not be troubled" or "have no fear" we can be sure that the people being addressed are in troubling and fearful situations.

From Moses to the apostles, the advice to "fear not" is sounded over and over again. When Moses was passing on his mission to deliver God's people to Canaan, he assured Joshua with these words: "It is the LORD who goes before you. He will be with you; he will not fail you or forsake you. Do not fear or be dismayed" (Deuteronomy 31:8). Joshua needed that message to be reinforced again and again as the people met with resistance in claiming the land (Joshua 1:9; 8:1; 10:25).

When God's people are in exile in Babylon, separated from the temple and the land God promised, they are unsure of their future. God assures them through Isaiah 41:10: "You are my servant, / I have chosen you and not cast you off; / do not fear, for I am with you, / do not be afraid, for I am your God." Jeremiah 46:27 also reminds God's people after many years in exile that they have nothing to fear: "But as for you, have not fear, my servant Jacob, / and do not be dismayed, O Israel; / for I am going to save you from far away, / and your offspring from the land of their captivity."

Mary, too, found herself troubled when the angel Gabriel showed up in Nazareth (Luke 1:26-38). Not only was Gabriel associated with the harrowing experiences of the end times in the Book of Daniel, he announced to Mary that she had found favor with God and would be overshadowed by the Spirit. As a faithful Jew, she would have known that anyone in their history favored by God was usually asked to do difficult things, and anyone overshadowed with God's spirit would suffer in the process. Yes, she was troubled, and given the assurance "The Lord is with you."

In fact, in almost every troubling situation in the Bible, the reason to have no fear is that God is present, God is accompanying his people, God is suffering with them, correcting them, protecting them, encouraging them. It is the reason that even on the verge of being arrested and put to death, Jesus could say to his closest followers at their last meal together, "Do not let your hearts be troubled. Believe in God, believe also in me" (John 14:1). Even then, he could leave them with a lasting gift: "Peace I leave with you; my peace I give to you. I do not give to you as the world gives. Do not let your hearts be troubled, and do not let them be afraid" (John 14:27).

It is a hallmark of our human journey that troubling situations and our natural responses of fear, anxiety, or worry reveal our need for God who is the source of peace. The peace that Jesus leaves with his followers is "not as the world gives." It is about wholeness and repairing what separates us from each other and from God. This peace requires our participation, our embrace of the things of God so that anything that binds us and others in misery will lose its power.

For Reflection:

- How might a "holy detachment" from fear, worry, and anxiety create an opening for God's peace in your life? In the lives of others?

- In what ways can we help others identify even the faintest longing for freedom in their lives? What messages from Scripture can bolster our own self-understanding and our ability to be a liberating force in the lives of others?

Afterword

What does this all mean for us? Slavery in the United States was abolished over 150 years ago, but its roots are sturdy. They are centuries old and span the globe.

Slavery grew in the soil of greed on the part of the "haves" and need on the part of the "have-nots." It flourished as economies became more and more dependent on cheap labor, and in cultures where there were few opportunities to move out of poverty. Selling oneself into slavery or indentured servitude, as was sometimes the case in biblical times and still occurs around the globe, is an act of desperation. It requires of those in the position to "purchase" such cheap labor a more creative and dignified response to poverty than to simply take advantage of circumstances that diminish other human beings.

Being sold into slavery to work plantations (as in American history) or build monuments (as in ancient imperial histories around the globe and into modern times), being torn from homelands and family, is participation in an evil that seems to have no end. The soil that supports such slavery is still greed but usually also adds in the fertilizer of racism. Rarely are people who look like "us" or talk like "us" devalued as easily as those who are "other," those who look different, who speak a different language, whose culture is unlike our own.

Yes, slavery may have been abolished at a historical point in time in America, but greed and racism are alive and well. To the extent that we are unaware of these dynamics, we participate in them. The gospel is good news to the extent that we allow it to transform us so that we can help to transform our world.

The church in Latin America often uses a three-step process to discern how to respond to what is happening in the world, and how God may be at work in it. The first step is to see, to commit to becoming aware of what is happening. The second step is to draw conclusions and choose a true and just way of thinking. The third step is to act, to put into action how God is at work and what God may be asking of us. On the issue of how the Bible addresses slavery and freedom, these steps might be particularly helpful.

We may be unaware, willfully or not, that human beings are "trafficked" every day right in our own nation, but we can inform ourselves. We can allow ourselves to be affected by the truth that young girls and women are often drugged and beaten and diminished in numerous ways so that they can be prostituted for the financial gain of their handlers. We can allow ourselves to be affected by the truth that men and women from other countries are often brought to our country with empty promises of jobs that can help their families, only to find themselves underpaid and barely able to subsist while their "employers" turn a handy profit. Investigate these and other forms of human slavery by visiting websites for the United Nations, the United States Department of State and Department of Justice, the offices of Attorneys General in your state, the

Migration Data Portal, Catholic Charities USA, the Jewish Council for Public Affairs, and many others.

If you are unaware of the extent to which practices and policies disproportionately affect some racial groups and not others, find ways to broaden your information base. Read about the history of Jim Crow laws or find out about historical events that occurred long after reconstruction that inflamed race relations (such as, the burning of destruction of lives and businesses in the Greenwood District in Tulsa, Oklahoma, or the treatment of Black American veterans of two world wars). Listen to one another's stories, especially seeking out opportunities to hear from people who are not part of your own racial group. This kind of mutual vulnerability and listening can become a vital part of our continuing conversion as God's people.

These are not easy things to do, but they are a necessary part of eradicating the greed and racism that still exist in our everyday world. If we believe the Bible's message that humans are made in God's image and likeness, then it is our duty to seek out that divine identity in each person. We see what has been happening and may still be happening that enslaves ourselves or others, and we prayerfully choose to think in ways that are consistent with the belief that God's very image is being damaged. Then, we ask for the grace to act in ways that will remove the influences of greed and racism. Perhaps this is the kind of service that is a sign of our ultimate freedom in Christ.

Notes

1. Emily Degn, "Top 10 Modern-Day Slavery Facts," April 9, 2018, https://borgenproject.org/top-10-modern-day-slavery-facts/.

2. Noel Rae, "How Christian Slaveholders Used the Bible to Justify Slavery," *Time*, February 23, 2018, https://time.com/5171819/christianity-slavery-book-excerpt/.

3. Archives of the Diocese of Georgia, An Episcopal Diocese of Georgia site, http://archives.georgiaepiscopal.org/?page_id=13.

4. Shannen Dee Williams, "Religious orders owning slaves isn't new—black Catholics have emphasized this history for years," *America*, August 6, 2019, https://www.americamagazine.org/faith/2019/08/06/religious-orders-owning-slaves-isnt-new-black-catholics-have-emphasized-history.

5. "Slavery, Memory, and Reconciliation," Georgetown University, http://slavery.georgetown.edu/.

6. Frederick Douglass, *Narrative of the Life of Frederick Douglass, An American Slave*, appendix, 1845, https://americanliterature.com/author/frederick-douglass/book/narrative-of-the-life-of-frederick-douglass-an-american-slave/appendix.

7. Michel Martin, "Slave Bible From The 1800s Omitted Key Passages That Could Incite Rebellion," first heard on All Things Considered, National Public Radio, transcript at npr.org, December 9, 2018, https://www.npr.org/2018/12/09/674995075/slave-bible-from-the-1800s-omitted-key-passages-that-could-incite-rebellion.

8. Yvette Alt Miller, "Passover: How Can We Identify with the Jewish Slaves Today?", *The Jewish Voice*, March 2020, https://thejewishvoice.com/2020/03/Passover-how-can-we-identify-with-the-jewish-slaves-today-2/.

9. "Trafficked: Three survivors of human trafficking share their stories," UN Women, July 29, 2019, https://www.unwomen.org/en/news/stories/2019/7/compilation-trafficking-survivors-share-stories.

10. Matthew Briand, "Finding Freedom in a Lockdown: The Common Good and Liberty Don't Have to be at Odds," first published in *Faith & Politics, In the News,* May 11, 2020, https://thejesuitpost. org/2020/05/finding-freedom-in-a-lockdownthe-common-good-and-liberty-dont-have-to-be-at-odds/.

11. Walter Brueggemann, *The Prophetic Imagination, 40th Anniversary Edition.* (Minneapolis: Fortress Press, 2018), chapter 1.

12. Kira Dault, "What is the Preferential Option for the Poor?", *U. S. Catholic,* January 22, 2015, https://uscatholic.org/articles/201501/ what-is-the-preferential-option-for-the-poor/.

13. Nelson Mandela, "The Oppressor and the Oppressed Must Both Be Liberated," from *Long Walk to Freedom,* accessed January 7, 2021, https://www.awakin.org/read/view.php?tid=2175.

14. Angelina Grimké, "An Appeal to the Christian Women of the South (1836)," in *Let Justice Be Done, Writings from the American Abolitionists 1688–1865,* ed. Kerry Walters (Maryknoll, NY: Orbis Books, 2020), 63.

15. Ibid.

16. Sarah Moore Grimké, *An Epistle to the Clergy of the Southern States* (1836), in *Let Justice Be Done, Writings from the American Abolitionists 1688–1865,* ed. Kerry Walters (Maryknoll, NY: Orbis Books, 2020), 69.

17. Ibid, pp. 70–71.

18. Karin Lehnardt, "56 Little-Known Trafficking Facts," August 2, 2019, https://www.factretriever.com/human-trafficking-facts.

19. Anthony J. Marsella, "The Golden Rule: Eleven World Religions," Transcend Media Service, October 9, 2017, https://www.transcend. org/tms/2017/10/the-golden-rule-eleven-world-religions/.

20. Kate Hakala, "What Happened to the Little Rock 9?", *Grunge,* June 16, 2020, https://www.grunge.com/218276/what-happened-to-the-little-rock-9/?utm_campaign=clip.

21. Melba Pattillo Beals, "How a Member of the Little Rock Nine Found Courage," *Guideposts,* June 28, 2018, https://www. guideposts.org/inspiration/inspiring-stories/stories-of-faith/how-a-member-of-the-little-rock-nine-found-courage.

22. Ibid.

23. Martin Luther King, "I Have a Dream" speech, August 28, 1963. Posted on Our Luther King website, January 1, 2019, https://ourlutherking.com/i-have-a-dream-speech-text/.

24. Ibid.

25. Brad R. Braxton, *No Longer Slaves, Galatians and African American Experience*. (Collegeville, MN: Liturgical Press, 2002), 2.

26. Francis de Sales, *Treatise on the Love of God*, 1616, Translated by Henry Benedict Mackey, OSB (Rockford, IL: Tan Publishing, 1997), Chapter V, 376. Available at https://www.catholicspiritualdirection.org/treatiseloveofgod.pdf .

New City Press

New City Press is one of more than 20 publishing houses sponsored by the Focolare, a movement founded by Chiara Lubich to help bring about the realization of Jesus' prayer: "That all may be one" (John 17:21). In view of that goal, New City Press publishes books and resources that enrich the lives of people and help all to strive toward the unity of the entire human family. We are a member of the Association of Catholic Publishers.

www.newcitypress.com
202 Comforter Blvd.
Hyde Park, New York

Periodicals
Living City Magazine
www.livingcitymagazine.com

Scan to join our mailing list
for discounts and promotions
or go to www.newcitypress.com
and click on "join our email list."